This book has helped lenges of those who came ᴵ. miraculous way the hardships and dangers which ᴜᵢₑy ᵢₐₑ daily basis."Against All Odds" is an appropriate title for this publication, and I'm convinced it will be of interest to young and old alike. The author's ability to bring these stories to life is a great gift that we will all benefit from. This book has helped me to understand the faith, courage, and dedication of those who did so much to establish this area.

Jack H. Goaslind, Manti Temple President
and emeritus General Authority.

If you find pleasure in stories based on true incidents, you'll love Against All Odds. Shirley Anderson Bahlmann spent the latter half of her childhood in the tradition-laden rural town of Manti, Utah. As a youth she absorbed the intrigue and mystique of early pioneer history and folklore. Her work stems from a deeply held reverence of the area's early beginnings. The resultant short stories are written in an easy-to-read, colorful, flowing narrative style. They can be read in solitude or orally around a campfire or in a living room for family and friends. This book makes an ideal gift for adults or children alike. It's content has a universal appeal reaching far beyond the locale of rural Utah. I found it to be a riveting read because of its interesting and distinctive content.

Coach Wilbur Braithwaite, Utah High School Coach
of the Year, National Coach Hall of Fame, 2002 Winter Olympic
torch bearer

This is a charming assortment of stories that brings pioneer times to life for modern families. The stories are written in such a way that I could see my children, my friends, and even myself facing the same problems today that are presented from the experiences of our forefathers.

.   *Ivo Ray Peterson, Mormon Miracle Pageant Director*

Through the eyes of Shirley's sometimes serious, sometimes humorous characters, the reader is able to experience some of the historical events of the early settlement of Utah. Some of these stories were familiar, but reading them in her witty penmanship brought these events to life with a desire to learn more.

Lannette Nielson, composer

A unique blend of historic fact skillfully woven in with captivating fiction. Inspiring!

Debbie Harman, professional artist

Against All Odds

Against All Odds

Amazing Pioneer Stories

of Courage and Survival

by

Shirley Bahlmann

BONNEVILLE BOOKS™

Springville, Utah

ISBN: 1-55517-590-2
v.1

Published by Bonneville Books
Imprint of Cedar Fort Inc.
www.cedarfort.com

Distributed by:

Typeset by Kristin Nelson
Cover design by Adam Ford
Cover design © 2001 by Lyle Mortimer

Printed in the United States of America
10 9 8 7 6 5 4 3 2 1

Printed on acid-free paper

    Library of Congress Cataloging-in-Publication Data

Bahlmann, Shirley A.
  Against All Odds: Amazing Pioneer Stories of Courage and Survival/ by Shirley A. Bahlmann.
      p. cm.
  ISBN 1-55517-590-2
  1. Mormon pioneers--West (U.S.)--Biography--Anecdotes. 2. Frontier
and pioneer life--West (U.S.)--Anecdotes. 3. Fortitude--Anecdotes. 4.
West (U.S.)--Biography--Anecdotes. I. Title.
  F593 .B14 2002
  978'.0088283--dc21
                            2001006571

For Momma Ru and Daddy Dell,
who showed me how to face all odds, and gave me
a wonderfully odd upbringing!

Thanks to Carol, Carolyn, Jerry, Keith,
Linda, LoDel, and Rebecca

for various help and encouragement that saw
this book to completion!

Table of Contents

Foreword

I first met Shirley as a Seventh Grade transplant from New Jersey when she enrolled in my French language class in Ephraim Jr. High School. While at best a mediocre student of languages, I recognized in her a creative intelligence and a passionate way of looking at the world and her role in it.

Not only a student of mine, Shirley was also my neighbor. We shared the common trait of not being native to Manti, since I was also a transplant, hailing from Belgium by way of Chicago. Yet we both came to share an interest in pioneer history.

After graduating from high school, Shirley assisted me on a Sanpete County history research project for my book *The Other 49ers*. Thus, I shared my own enthusiasm for my adopted Utah history and unwittingly began Shirley on the trail that ultimately led to the creation of this book.

One or two of these stories occurred within an arrow's shot of my own house. But anyone who has ridden through the rugged and beautiful western landscape can easily imagine the settings for these vivid and moving stories.

Shirley has researched some of the most interesting life-or-death situations that I have known of from pioneer times. Stories that can take your imagination into situations that you can't seem to see your way out of, and when danger is at last conquered, you can't help but feel relief and amazement at the outcome.

I appreciate the timelessness of these tales, told with a regional flavor that richly colors these anecdotes from my adopted home.

Albert Antrei, author,
educator, historian

*Following each chapter
is a brief explanation
of which elements
of the story are true.*

Strange Bedfellows

They always came in the dark, like nightmares. Through the window, I saw their painted faces, flickering like demons in the torchlight. The shadows danced and crawled across their angry features as if they had lives of their own.

Trembling, I slid down under the window and covered my eyes. But I could still hear them. Their voices were low and muffled, a threatening buzzing sound, like bees upset from their hive.

I could smell the smoke from their torches, implements of torture that they used to start houses and sometimes people on fire.

Any second now they would reach the front door. They would pound it, smash the wood, break it down. They would swarm through the house, breaking dishes, tearing books, throwing bedcovers off to look underneath, ripping out clothes to search wardrobes. They would find me. They would grab me by the hair and drag me outside, thumping my body down the bare wooden steps, laughing at my pain. They would beat me, unless I could escape.

My eyes snapped open as fear yanked me awake and pushed me upright. My heart hammered painfully, my breathing was fast. My legs were twitching to run until I caught sight of my mother bending over a cooking fire at the mouth of the dugout. I could smell the lingering torch smoke, but it came from the cooking fire, not the mob. The hated mob was gone.

When I saw that I was safe, the fear leaked out of my muscles and I fell back onto my bed of blankets, trembling.

The mobs with their smoking torches, guns, knives, sickening burning hot tar and feathers were a thousand miles away in Illinois and Missouri. They were too cowardly to follow us across the wilderness to Utah, to this place called Manti. They would never find me in this dugout, those evil, shrivel hearted people, who hated us Mormons for no reason.

We had done nothing to them, yet they burned our homes, beat us, stole from us, and drove us out. I had seen them strip people, scorch their screaming bodies with burning hot tar that stuck like a second skin, then stick feathers to the tar for further humiliation. When the tar was eventually peeled off the victim by loving friends and family, skin usually came off, too.

Those mobs were worse than the Indians. Even though both groups painted their faces, took prisoners, and were cruel to their enemies, the Indians were more honorable than those hated mobs. If the Ute Indians attacked, you knew it was them, and they didn't pretend it wasn't. They did not deny it. Fighting was their way of life.

The mobs disguised themselves so that after their night of evil acts, they could go to church the next day. They would smile, greet their neighbors, and entertain in their parlors. If they heard about the burnings and killings, those horrid hypocrites would act surprised, as though they knew nothing about it.

I thought of Papa, and then angrily rubbed my stinging eyes. Crying wouldn't bring him back no matter how much I missed him. It still twisted my insides in knots and made me feel sick when I remembered his gentle face contorted with fear as the mob dragged him out of our house and out of my life forever.

2

At Papa's funeral, Bishop Whitmer said we should forgive our enemies. He said Papa was joyfully serving our Lord and Savior, and was far from the pain, sorrow, and toil of this life. I could not get past my own misery to feel joy for my father. I could not wait to leave that hellish place and those vicious people.

I smiled a hard little smile to myself as I remembered overhearing Sister Siddons say to Mama, "That Annie of yours works like a boy!" I knew I had worked long and tirelessly to get our handcart ready. I did it because I had to get out of that place of evil. Mama had never been the same since Papa was taken from us. She couldn't seem to decide what to do unless I told her. It wasn't that she was weak-minded. She was just scared. I don't think she would have gone on the trek to Utah if I hadn't insisted. She followed me across the rivers, plains, and through the mountain passes.

Any time I felt hot, tired, hungry, dirty, itchy, sick, or scared while walking and walking and walking to get to Salt Lake City, I repeated to myself, "We're going to a better place. We're going to a better place." It helped me to make it. I felt like I could do anything. Being a girl could not stop me. Being thirteen years old could not stop me. Being hungry and cold could not stop me.

When we got to Salt Lake City, there wasn't much there. I was happy to dig in and help, for when I was working hard, I didn't have time to re-live my horrible memories.

Then a Ute Indian chief named Walkara, or Walker as some settlers called him, came to Salt Lake City and told Brigham Young he wanted him to send some settlers to San Pitch, in central Utah. He said he would welcome the white man to this valley, to teach his people farming and the white man's ways. When President Young decided to send settlers, he asked for volunteers. I convinced Mama that we should go. It's hard to explain, but it seemed as if I could get to a brand new place, where no one had settled before, I could finally feel safe.

It was cold November when we got to the barren valley. Mama and I settled in a dugout on the south side of a hill. Bishop Morley said the hill would be used for building a temple. Most of the other families made dugouts, too. It was hard work to get our dugouts large enough to live in. The Cox's wanted us to move into theirs, but I said no. I'd had enough of people being able to watch me walk, eat, sleep, scratch myself, blow my nose, and do my private business on the trek. Now I wanted walls. I needed walls. It didn't matter if they were wood, brick, rock or dirt, just so they were walls.

Mama helped dig out the dirt to enlarge our primitive little home. She stopped when she was tired. I kept working. Some of the men helped us, which was fine with me, but I didn't ask them for their help. We finally had our own place, Mama and me.

A few other families simply tipped their wagons over and put a tarp over the top keep out the snow. It was easier than digging, but I secretly thought the dugout was better. There were no drafts at the back, and when the sun was out it shone right into our place, warming things up and lifting my spirits.

As the cold, bitter winter of 1849-50 wore on, the wagon tippers realized what poor shelters they had against the elements, and many of them moved into dugouts, too.

Now that the winter was almost over, I was thankful the past two weeks had been steadily warming up. It felt like spring was finally, really and truly, coming to this wild valley. I was filled with a renewed determination to get started on a cabin

4

for my mother and me. I'd never built a house before, but I told myself I could do it.

After our meager breakfast, I went out to the spot where Mama's and my house would be. I had borrowed a shovel. I wasn't sure who's it was, but it didn't really matter, because we all shared pretty much everything.

I struggled through the sticky mud, which sucked and pulled at my high-buttoned shoes. I traced a shallow trench for what I thought was a pretty good house. It was not too big because Mama and me didn't need much. I imagined where the kitchen would be, and in my mind I put a bed in the farthest corner, on the east side where the sun would wake us up in the morning.

I felt better when I was done, as did I always when carrying out a plan. That night I went to bed with a light heart.

I woke up to an eerie gray stillness. A sense of unease and foreboding had replaced my earlier optimism. Although this morning was the warmest one yet, I thought that if I built a fire, it might shake off the bad feeling I had. Just doing something normal and routine should help me feel better. I got up quietly so as not to wake Mama, built a tinder pile in the cooking pit, and then reached for a smooth stick that I could see out of the corner of my eye. When I grabbed it, it moved. I yanked my hand back and screamed. I stared at the "stick," horrified as it coiled up and raised its head. It was a snake!

Mama sat up from her blanket pile. "What is it?" she asked. "Snake!" I squealed. When I heard the panic in my voice, I was embarrassed. I told myself to calm down, that I had been through much worse in my life than a snake.

I noticed my mother's blanket moving, and thought she was

5

getting up to help me. Then I realized that she was sitting stock-still, staring down in silent, horror-stricken fascination at a crawling, twisting pile of snakes writhing on her lap.

An urgent need to protect my mother prompted me to action. I grabbed the bottom edge of her quilt and pulled it off of her, then dragged it out of the cave opening, rolling it down the hill with a swift kick of my foot.

"Rattlesnakes," Mama said, standing up in her nightgown and nightcap. "They're poisonous." She looked frail and child-like, standing there, wringing her hands, and biting her lip to keep from crying.

I was angry. We had been through enough. I grabbed the shovel I'd used the day before, and I hit the snake lying beside the cooking pit over and over again until I was sure that it was dead. Then I scooped it up and threw it out of the dugout.

As I turned to go back inside, a snake plopped down on the ground next to me. I cringed and looked up. Squirming out of the cracks in the ledge above our dugout were more rattlesnakes. Some of them dripped down the sides of the rocks like pus out of an infected wound. Some dropped to the ground where they landed in the dugout doorway forming a writhing, twisted pile. They were too cold to move fast, but they were moving.

I thought of the plagues of Egypt from the Bible. What had we done so wrong? Hadn't we suffered enough? What did God want from us? My jaw clenched. My muscles tightened. I was too angry to cry or even to feel scared. I lifted my shovel again, and beat at the pile of snakes. I hit the ones on the rocks until they fell to the ground. I hardly thought about what I was doing. I just knew I had to protect my mother, and that nothing must happen to her. I needed her.

I heard some screams, and almost told Mama that it was all right, we'd be all right, we had to be all right, when I realized the screams were coming from the other dugouts. There was shouting, and banging. Mama stepped cautiously to the mouth of the dugout, shuddering at the snake bodies spread on the ground.

"There are more of them," she said almost hopelessly. "They're everywhere." I didn't have to guess what "they" were. It could only be snakes.

The first onslaught of snakes was killed in a couple of hours. Other people in the settlement were piling them up outside of their dugouts, too. Throughout that day, snakes would slither out of a crack, a partially-opened dresser drawer, or maybe out from under a blanket. We were constantly vigilant and did not relax, even when the sun started to go down.

The Indians had been watching our unusual behavior from their camp. Chief Walkara, along with some braves and squaws, came over to see what new and strange activity these pale-faced people were doing.

His dark face fascinated me as I watched him approach the hill. When he caught sight of the snake piles, his eyes lit up and shone like black stars.

"You have many great snakes," he complimented Isaac Morley, our settlement leader and bishop who was often fondly addressed as "Father Morley."

"Yes, too many snakes," replied Father Morley.

"You no want, we take," Walkara said eagerly.

"You want these snakes? What for?"

"Plenty good. We eat, use skins, much good snakes."

Father Morley spread his hands toward the snakes. "They're yours," he smiled.

7

The chief gave a curt order to his Indians in their language. His underlings gathered the dead snakes onto hides with sticks, then folded up the corners of the hides and carried them away. I found out later that even dead snakes can bite. It's a reflex action, but it's just as poisonous as if they're alive.

I hate to admit that my Plagues of Egypt complaint was unjustified. No one was bitten by the three hundred snakes that were killed that day. When the infestation was over, about five hundred snakes were dead. They had been found everywhere, in people's beds, clothing, even cooking pots.

It was a blessing that everyone survived the spring awakening of hundreds of poisonous serpents, but another benefit was the Indians. Getting a feast of snakes from us put the Indians in such a good mood that they helped us with our spring planting.

I repented of my anger toward God. I finally understood what "blessing in disguise" meant.

The first settlers to Manti arrived in November and built dugouts in what is now Temple Hill to shelter them for the winter. In the spring, rattlesnakes coming out of winter hibernation crawled through the dugouts. The pioneers killed about 500 snakes, and the Indians were glad to receive them as gifts.

Buffalo Tag

"Wake up, Sloppy Joe," I said as I poked my finger into my twin brother's ear. He jerked his head away and flailed his arms as though to ward off a whole swarm of horseflies. I laughed as he opened his eyes, sat up, and glared at me.

"Why should I, Miss Maggie Messy?" he said testily.

"Because if you don't, all the soda bread will be gone, and you won't get any breakfast."

Joe moaned and fell back onto his blanket. "If I have to eat any more soda bread, I think I will die," he groaned.

"You'll definitely die if you don't eat," I retorted.

"I'll eat something else," Joe said in a small, hopeful voice.

"Help yourself," I said smugly. "There's plenty of grass growing here beside the trail. I'm sure the horses and oxen won't mind sharing."

Joe covered up his face with his blanket, and I got up and walked over to the fire where Ma was patting the mixture of flour, water, baking soda, and a little salt if Ma remembered, into flat little discs. As much as I teased Joe about the soda bread that we had to eat since our supplies were running dangerously low, I didn't relish the thought of eating it any more than he did. I just had to pretend I didn't care because then it bothered him more.

Ma was never careful about getting all the bugs out of the flour. The resulting hard, flat cakes were often speckled with insect parts. They were hard to chew and had a tang from the soda that left a bad aftertaste. The only thing that kept me from despair was that the mountains were in sight. We were almost to Zion.

"Margaret, please get me some water," Ma said as she plunked a piece of soda dough into the hot pan supported over the fire on a couple of flat rocks. She pushed her hair back off her forehead with the back of her hand. Even though it was a moderately cool morning, Ma's face was red and sweating from working beside the fire. Ma looked up at me and smiled hopefully. "Don't you think you're old enough to start pinning your hair up?"

I shook my head hard, enjoying the feel of the braid that danced down my back. I could also feel the loose hair that had pulled out of the braid tickling my face and neck as I slept. I imagined that I did look rather messy. But I also felt free. If I had my way, I'd never be old enough for stiff corsets and hard pins to scrape my head in the effort to create ridiculous, elaborate hairdos.

I took pity on my mother and picked up the wooden pail that sat beside our handcart, then made my way over to the stream beside our camp. The water rolled and chuckled in the early morning light, and I took the liberty of sticking my feet into it. I gasped at the cold, but relished the clean feeling of the water running over my dusty bare feet, swirling in between my tired toes and washing away all the fatigue that was left over from spending another night sleeping on the ground. Once we reached the promised land, the Zion of Salt Lake City, I would have a bed to sleep on again.

I sighed as the smell of scorched soda bread reached my nose, and lowered the bucket into the water, careful to dip it upstream from my dirty feet, and lugged it over to our camp-fire. Joe was sitting by Ma, forlornly picking at his portion of soda bread. Just as I let the bucket thud to the ground, I heard shouting.

"Buffalo!"

"Buffalo! C'mon, men!"

"Get your rifles!"

The camp jumped to life as several of the men grabbed their guns and jumped on their horses. I was amazed to see them ride toward a herd of buffalo that was leisurely grazing out from behind a hill on the opposite stream bank. I had just been sitting there and hadn't noticed them.

The nearest bison raised their dark, shaggy heads and looked curiously at the hunters as they splashed across the stream. They seemed interested, but not particularly alarmed.

Joe appeared at my side, looking triumphant. "There's your answer to this old soda bread!" he said, waving his scorched brown bread disc under my nose.

"Don't count your buffalo before they're skinned," I said.

"Aw, what do you know?" Joe said impatiently. "I could throw a rock and hit one from here!"

"You only wish you could," I said.

"Well, I'm not going to prove it to you. I might mess up the hunt," Joe said stoutly.

Then, seeing the scowl on his face and feeling sorry that I'd spoken unkindly, I said, "Let's go closer."

We walked together to the edge of the stream and watched the hunters approach the herd. If the buffalo didn't spook and run, we would be able to see the whole hunt from where we stood. I felt my mouth water and my stomach rumble at the thought of fresh meat roasting on our fire. One of those huge buffalo would feed the whole camp. Two would probably get us to Salt Lake City.

I jumped as Henry Shomaker's rifle suddenly exploded a bullet from its barrel, then saw the buffalo that was his target, the biggest one in the herd. I also saw a puff of dust kick up on the ground just beyond the big, shaggy bull. My heart sank with disappointment. Brother Shomaker had missed!

Then, faster than I would have thought an animal as big and heavy as that one could move, the old bull took off running at Brother Shomaker, its head lowered as it pointed its heavy black horns directly at horse and rider. I clutched Joe's sleeve and pointed.

"Turn the horse, turn the horse, turn the horse," Joe advised rapidly under his breath as Brother Shomaker hesitated. It seemed a long time, although it was really only a couple of seconds, before Brother Shomaker finally twisted on his saddle in a desperate turn, and the horse followed his lead, needing no urging to gallop as fast as she could away from the shaggy black menace that was chasing her with appallingly sharp horns.

Brother Shomaker kept glancing back over his shoulder at the buffalo that was hot on his trail. I was close enough to see the fear on his face, his mouth open in mute disbelief, his eyes wide as they cast behind him, then darted forward as though desperately seeking an escape route that hadn't been there the last time he looked.

The bull seemed to be closing in. What his wickedly pointed horns and sheer weight could do to a person, I didn't even want to imagine. Still holding onto Joe's shirt, I clasped my hands together for a brief, desperate prayer, "Oh, please help him," I breathed.

"Amen," said Joe, his eyes glued to the terrified rider.

Then I screamed. It was a short scream that just sort of squeezed out of me when I saw Brother Shomaker vault off his horse and land in a rolling heap on the hard prairie floor. He tumbled along until he hit into a large clump of grass, then he collapsed and lay still. I held my breath as the buffalo approached the fallen man. Then I let it out again in a big whoosh of relief as the huge beast thundered past Brother Shomaker, his eye and his aim on the unfortunate horse.

I didn't know if Brother Shomaker was dead, but I saw a couple of the mounted men riding toward him. I knew there was nothing I could do for him, so I let my eyes follow the horse.

Mouth open, hooves pounding, mane twisting in the artificial wind created by her speed, the horse tried vainly to outrun the angry buffalo. As soon as the big bull drew close enough, he stabbed his lowered horns into the horse's backside and gave a mighty toss of his massive head. The horse flipped up and over in a perfect somersault.

His attackers dispatched, the bull turned and trotted back to the center of the herd, seemingly satisfied that he had done a good day's work.

The horse struggled pitifully and finally got up, limping her way as fast as she could toward camp and the companionship of the other riderless horses. Brother Shomaker was brought in on the back of Brother Dayton's horse. He was bruised, scraped, and shaken up, but not broken.

His horse was worse off. She had deep cuts where the buffalo horns had gouged her flanks. She was bruised and skittish. Her wounds were doctored, and she eventually recovered. She had to be led riderless along the trail when we finally took up our journey again.

We had a slight delay as we cut up buffalo meat and smoked it on our campfires. The smell alone was almost enough to sustain me for the rest of the trek to Salt Lake City.

I did learn one thing. Never tease a buffalo. They have no sense of humor. Just like some people I know.

When charged by a buffalo on the prairie, a hunter leaped off his galloping horse in an effort to escape. The horse got flipped in a somersault when the buffalo tossed it with his horns. The horse and rider both survived.

Bloody Finger

I tried to work the sliver out with my fingernails, but it was in too deep. My finger was really starting to hurt.

I had felt the sliver go in when I hurried to grab up the firewood for the cook stove earlier that morning, but ignored it. It had seemed more important to get away to my friend Ann Olsen's than to get out a little sliver. Being the oldest of five children, and a girl at that, made me the most likely to get more chores if Mama thought of any before I left. I had to hurry!

Mama had let me deliver diaper flannel to the Olsen's, and I was happy to do it so I could visit Ann. Now the mile home was growing longer than the mile I'd walked to Olsen's. I trudged down the dusty trail in my long hot skirt, shaking my head at the flies that buzzed around my sweaty face. I could have borrowed the Olsen's needle to dig out the sliver, if they still had one. Needles were precious and easy to lose. But I hadn't even thought to ask.

My miserable reverie was broken by the sound of pounding feet and a strange gagging sound. Startled, I twisted around to look behind me, my heart jumping, until I saw that it was just Will Jorgensen lumbering along the track toward me. He was running a wobbly course, and he kept swiping his hand at his eyes as he ran. He didn't seem to be able to see very well, for he would occasionally crash his big leg through a gray-green sagebrush by the side of the trail. It did not even slow him down.

Alarmed by his behavior, I wondered whether he was being

attacked by bees or if he had been bitten by a rattlesnake and was going crazy from the poison. I didn't know much about rattlesnakes except that the first people that settled San Pitch Valley had killed a whole pile of them after they arrived.

Will was a big bully. I had seen him mimicking lame old Brother Hancock's crooked walk. I thought it was tragic that Brother Hancock had to have part of his frozen feet cut off at Winter Quarters. Will was mean to me, too, calling me names when no adults were around. He pushed little kids who got in his way. I had seen him throw rocks at dogs, even though President Brigham Young had told us to be kind to animals.

It surprised me to see big, mean Will run past me with what looked like tears running down his face! The gagging noise sounded more and more like crying. He didn't even seem to see me, which was unusual since I was the only other person in sight on the sagebrush flat. I had never seen Will act like this. My slivered finger forgotten, I walked faster, but still couldn't catch up to Will. I wanted to tell my mother what had happened.

Mama was a small, smiling, busy woman. I took after Papa, and had already grown taller than her. Her good nature was contagious. Even after crossing the plains with her six children, doing her best to provide for us from the supplies in a small handcart, and suffering the heartbreak of our baby brother Martin dying along the way, she still had a joy for living. I wondered what she would say about Will.

As soon as I got home, I reached for the latchstring that was supposed to be threaded through the small hole in the door. The string was attached to a crossbar that held the door closed on the inside. But the latchstring, which was really a strand of leather, wasn't there, so I couldn't pull the crossbar out of the metal bracket to get the door open. As I stared at the empty hole, which was about as big around as a finger, I felt a flash of irritation. Ned or Sam was playing tricks on me again.

"Let me in!" I called through the hole as I pounded on the door. After a few seconds, Ned pulled the door open. One look at his pale, somber face changed my mind about yelling at him. I couldn't remember the last time he had been so scared. I felt uneasy as I glanced around the room and saw our mother sitting on a chair, looking at the floor.

"What's wrong?" I asked fearfully, my stomach tightening as I imagined little Rosalie deathly ill, or Samuel having fallen down the well and broken an important bone. "Oh, Carrie," she whispered, "Indians."

I was confused. The Indians had originally welcomed us. I still wasn't used to them, even though they occasionally came to our homes, especially on baking day. They really liked our bread.

Mama followed Brigham Young's advice and would give them bread or old clothes if she had any. I wondered if the Indians had come and taken all our food while I was gone to Olsen's. "Indians?" I said stupidly.

"They killed some men who were working in the fields this morning," Mother put her hands up to cover her eyes.

"Who?" I asked, my heart squeezing painfully in a sudden spasm, "Not. . . ?"

"No, not your father," Mother quickly replied. "It was Brother Meade and young Simon Jorgensen."

I sank to the floor, my knees weak with relief and dread, and wondered just how it had happened. I imagined thin, old, dour-looking Mr. Meade out working in the fields in his faded brown hat, and Simon Jorgensen, eighteen years old, with a square, pleasant face and a wry humor, who'd only come to our settlement last winter.

I couldn't help wondering about the details. Were the two men hoeing? Changing irrigation water? Did the Indians sneak up, or did they charge down on their horses, hollering? Were the men scared? Why did the Indians do it? Did they want to steal something? Was it revenge for something we didn't even know we did wrong? Were they in a bad mood? Would they attack again? Would they come to my house?

My whirling thoughts settled on the fact that Simon had moved here to live with his older brother, Lars, who was Will's father. Simon was Will's uncle. Being so close to Will's age, though, he'd been more like a big brother to him. Now Will's behavior this morning made sense! Poor Will. I never thought I'd feel sorry for that bully.

Perhaps my slumped posture, or the look on my face triggered some resolve inside my mother, for she got up briskly and, although shorter than me, put out a hand to help me to my feet. I winced as she squeezed the slivered finger. After a brief examination, she went to fetch the needle. I hardly felt it as she dug the offending bit of wood out. Some things in life were worse than a sliver.

Just about everyone from town was at the funeral the next morning. The men stood around the outer edges of the gathering with their rifles in their hands, although I personally doubted whether the Indians would interrupt a funeral. I'd heard that they were very particular about not desecrating burial places, even those of their enemies.

I sneaked a glance at Will, who was standing close to his mother, his head bowed. He looked oddly like a small child in a too-large body, and seemed to want to hide behind his mother's dress. He kept swiping his hands at his eyes in an irritated, almost angry way.

Bishop Allred talked about Angus Meade and Simon Jorgensen going together like missionaries into the next life, and having work to do there. He said that Heavenly Father needed them more than we did, and that they were happy and wanted us to be happy, too. By the time he was done speaking, I did believe that Brother Meade and Simon were in a better place, but I still felt sorry for their families left behind.

I looked at my father, so much taller than Mother that she barely reached his shoulder, and I imagined that it could have been him killed. I did not feel happy, even when we sang "Come, Come, Ye Saints," one of my favorite songs.

After the brief funeral, Papa said he was going to work in the fields. Mother looked at him in alarm.

"Today? Oh, Joseph!" she exclaimed.

"The fields must be tended and watered," he replied. "We must do our part, and the Lord will protect me or take me, whatever His will is. I could die standing right here, if it were His will. Remember, the Lord has a plan, and He is in charge. We need to go on with life as usual."

Mother embraced him, clasping his waist with her strong, slender arms. "You're not going alone?" she asked.

"No, the brethren decided that we should work in groups, with our guns at our sides," Father replied.

Mother wouldn't let any of us go outside, and eight-year-old Thelma didn't want to. Petite like our mother, she was quite a homebody. But unlike Mother, Thelma was timid and did not seek people out. She was content to sit at the table by the front door, peeling potatoes so Mother could make a fresh batch of sourdough starter out of potato water. Sam had accidentally thrown the last batch of sourdough start out the door, thinking it was sour mush. He decided that if he got rid of it, he wouldn't have to eat it. The starter was used like yeast to make bread rise light and airy before it was baked.

Some of the potatoes would also go into a venison stew for dinner with enough extra to take to the Meade and Jorgensen families after Papa got home.

Mother wouldn't even let Sam go out to the outhouse, telling him to use the chamber pot in the cabin corner. The little ones got restless, whining and pulling hair and crying. I also felt trapped in our small adobe house. The two windows seemed very small. They were covered with oiled paper, which was much cheaper than glass, but you couldn't see through it.

I felt as though I needed air, and offered to take the children outside for a few minutes. Mother looked up at me with intense, searching eyes, and finally consented after I agreed to stay right by the house. I gratefully pulled up the latch and opened the door.

The summer heat hit my face as I led the children into the yard. Our adobe house stayed cool even in the summer, because the thick walls of dried mud kept out most of the heat. Rosalie burst out into the sunshine, her two-year-old legs running to the shade of the young Russian Olive tree by our house and plopping down in the dirt. Sam pulled out the stick horse Father had helped him make from a tree branch with some dried grass for a mane and tail. He began galloping around the house, but not for long because it was a hot afternoon. I was glad that Pettyville almost always cooled off at night from an evening breeze that wound its way down the canyon, blowing a cool breath across the valley.

We sat peacefully for a while, a few buzzing flies disturbing the quiet, until Sam stood up and pointed. "Horses!" he yelled excitedly. I wondered who was coming to visit. We didn't have a lot of horses. Most of us had arrived here by handcart, but there were some work horses and a few buggy pullers. I looked toward the veil of dust that was rapidly growing larger. It made me uneasy. It was coming from the mountains, not the fields or the direction of other houses in the settlement.

I suddenly called to Sam and ran over to snatch up Rosalie. Sam was reluctant to leave the yard, because he wanted to see the horses, which he loved. Ned opened the door before I could grab the latchstring. "Indians!" I almost sobbed at Ned's startled face. Mama overheard me. Her mouth a grim, straight line, she took Rosalie out of my arms and laid her on the big bed. Mama smiled at her and said, "You and Sam can play ships!" Sam bounded onto the bed and announced that he was captain. That was fine with Rosalie, who was perfectly content to be crew, passengers, or even a fish if that's what Sam wanted her to be.

Mama called me to help her move the washtub in front of the door. It was a meager effort to block the door, since even I could have pushed it aside if I had wanted to. As Mama straightened from pulling the washtub into place, I saw her lips moving, and guessed that she was praying. Her eyes lit on the latchbar and the leather string that snaked out of the small hole. She reached out and pulled the string to the inside, leaving the bar resting in its iron arm, securely blocking the wooden door. She walked quickly around the single room, pausing in front of each window to fasten the wooden shutters and listen. The house darkened, but a little light still leaked through the windows. "Get under the bed," she said suddenly. Sam and Rosalie thought this was a fine new game. Ned helped by saying, "Let's pretend we're in a cave!" Thelma was much less enthusiastic, but tucked herself in under the headboard, obedient as usual.

By then, there was not enough room for me. We could distinctly hear the hoofbeats drawing rapidly closer. My heart began to pound. This was real. We were not pretending. The Indians had killed two men yesterday, and now they were here, at our house.

"Hide!" Mother commanded me, in an unusually high-pitched voice. I ducked under the kitchen table next to the front door. The horses stopped their rhythmic hoofbeats and began stepping quietly around in front of our house. I heard softer footfalls approaching, and listened as they circled the cabin, pausing at the windows.

Mother had flattened herself against the wall by the door, and jumped when the door suddenly vibrated with powerful hammering. Loud, heavy voices yelled something I could not understand.

I could hardly breathe and covered my ears with my hands and squeezed my knees between my elbows, but I couldn't stop staring at the door. I felt tight and scared inside. It seemed to me that by watching the door, I could somehow will it to stay closed and keep the danger outside.

The pounding stopped and the footfalls made their way around the cabin again, pausing at the windows as before. I could hear what sounded like arguing. The footsteps made their way to the front door again. I found myself praying that they would just go away and not hurt us. *Please go away. Papa, come home!*

Then I thought I heard laughter. It startled me. I did not see anything funny about our situation. It was strange to hear someone laughing when the fear I felt made me sick inside. I looked at the door, then almost choked on my fear. A dark, brown finger was poking through the latchstring hole and was feeling its way along the wooden bar where the string was attached. If that probing finger found the latchstring, it could pull it back through the hole and open the door!

I was so fixed on the horrifying sight that I didn't notice what my mother was doing until I saw her raise a large knife in her hands and bring it down on the finger with such force that it was completely severed from the hand in one blow. A loud scream from outside pierced my reserve, and I screamed, too, and began to shake. I heard screaming and crying from under the bed. Staring at the bloody brown finger on the floor, I started to cry.

The horses galloped away. As the sound of their hoof beats faded in the distance, I crawled out from under the table and found my mother leaning against the wall with her eyes closed and tears running down her cheeks. I grabbed her in a desperate hug, and it seemed to break whatever spell she was under.

She moved to the window, listened intently, then walked over to the bed and called the children out from under it. She fell down onto the comforter. Rosalie scrambled up to snuggle by Mother's side, Thelma climbed up and stroked her hand. Sam and Ned stared at the finger on the floor. "Mother, you are so brave!" Ned exclaimed in awe.

As Mother held her daughters, Ned used the stove poker to push the finger to the edge of the door. He quickly opened it, shoved the finger out, and slammed the door again. He led Sam by the hand to join us on the bed.

It was nearly dark when Papa got home from the fields. He listened to garbled accounts of the incident from several voices at once, then understood what had happened. He inspected the bloody stain on the floor, then scrubbed it with ashes and lye. He scraped and scrubbed until he got the stain out for Mama. His grave face looked around at each one of us, and he had us all kneel down and say a prayer of gratitude for our safety.

The next day, Papa didn't go to the fields. He began making adobes for an addition to the cabin. Ned and I helped set out the wooden block forms, mix the clay-like mud with straw to help hold the finished bricks together, and then added water from the well. We shoveled the mixture into the molds with satisfying plops. When they were all filled, we had to stop to let the bricks dry before we took the wooden frames off. That could take a week or more, depending on the weather.

Papa moved over to the dried logs he'd dragged down to the house from the river bottom and began cutting firewood. Ned and I hauled the cut wood to the woodpile.

Thelma came around the house and called to us to come and eat, then made a little choking sound. We looked up, wondering if she was all right. She was staring at the mountains. As I turned to follow her gaze, I felt my stomach clench. A dust cloud was working its way toward us. It looked just like the dust cloud from the day before. I momentarily felt courage that Papa was there, but then I realized that though he was big and strong, he could be killed just like Brother Meade and Simon Johansen.

"In the house," Papa said tersely. I was already on my way. I could only imagine what the Indians would do to us in revenge for cutting off one of their fingers. They couldn't set our adobe house on fire, because adobe wouldn't burn, but our front door was made of wood. I just hoped Papa knew what to do. He was right behind me as I quickly followed Ned through the door. "Lord help us," I heard him mutter.

Just like a nightmare, I heard the horse's hooves draw closer to our house until they stopped. My heart was squeezed so tight in fear, I wondered if it would hurt any worse to have an Indian arrow shot into it.

I crouched on the floor with Sam and Ned on either side, Rosalie on my lap. Thelma sat by Ned, clutching his arm and hiding her face in his shoulder.

Mama stood in front of us, the knife held firmly in her hand. The stiffness in her back reflected the look of grim determination she wore on her face. A small measure of comfort filled me knowing that she would defend us to the death. I bit my lip to keep from crying out loud. I did not want my mother dead!

Papa stood by the door, his rifle in his hands.

The footsteps did not go around the cabin like the day before. They walked up to the front door and then a knock sounded. There was no imperative hammering on the wood. I figured it could be a trick. Papa looked back at us, his eyes intense but unafraid. Then he turned back to the door.

I wanted to call out, "No!" when I saw Papa reach for the latch, but before my dry throat could form a sound, he'd opened the door wide enough that he could see out. I heard a guttural voice that spoke halting English say, "Where brave woman, cut off Indian finger?"

"What do you want with her?" Papa demanded.

"See brave woman. Good medicine," was the reply.

There was a long moment of silence. Then Papa opened the door all the way and called, "Elizabeth." Mother walked over and stood by him.

As he moved aside to make room for her in the doorway, I saw a dark brown face just outside the opening, with long black hair hanging down either side. There was a feather cocked sideways, sticking out from behind his head. His chest was bare, his mouth was held in a firm, straight line, but his dark eyes looked admiringly at my mother and took a lively interest in the knife

25

she still clutched in her hand.

"Heap brave," he said respectfully as he held out his hand, which had some kind of wrapping that looked like leather with brown mossy packing sticking out the sides. Only three fingers and a thumb poked out from the primitive bandage.

His gesture was similar to what he'd seen white men do when they shake hands, but with the palm up. Mama glanced up at Papa, who nodded encouragingly at her. With the knife-free hand, Mother reached out and touched the Indian's upturned palm, below the bandage. He seemed satisfied, as though it were good medicine just to have her touch him. He moved aside, and another Indian appeared in the doorway, slightly shorter, a bit heavier, but also with a feather in his greasy black hair, and saying, "Heap brave," as he extended his hand toward Mother. So it went, until every Indian in the raiding party of the day before had complimented Mother on her bravery and had a chance to touch her hand. Then they all got on their horses and I heard them ride away.

I got up with all the children and we embraced our parents. Papa had us kneel down right then and there, and offer up a prayer of thanks for our safety.

The Indians never bothered us again. There were times when they were in a bad mood, or angry, and attacked people, but not anyone at our house. The other mothers in the settlement would bring their children to our house for safety if they heard that the Indians were on the warpath. Their children were always safe in the home of "Heap brave woman."

A woman alone at home with her children in Pettyville (now a ghost town) cut off the finger of an Indian who was part of a raiding party when he tried to lift the door latch

26

through the latch string hole. The next day the Indians returned to the house and praised the woman for her bravery, each one wanting to touch her for "good medicine." When they felt the need, other pioneer mothers brought their children to her house for safety because the Indians never bothered her or her household again.

Savage Samaritan

I blew on my fingers to try to warm them up, but even my breath felt cold. I hunkered down by the small campfire.

"John!" I jumped up and whirled guiltily. My grandfather's icy blue eyes were fixed on me. "We need to make another wood run!" he snapped impatiently. As I left the only spot of warmth I had in the whole world, resentment seeped into my heart like cold into my clothes. I resented my father who had forced me to go on this adventure with a grandfather I barely knew.

Salt Canyon, east of Fort Nephi, had become my whole world since the supply wagons had gotten stuck in the blizzard. The snow was clear up past the wagon boxes and deeper than the wheels. It was frozen so hard, it would take a team of twenty horses to pull the wagons out.

Grandfather had thought of making shelters by digging a doorway out of the snow from under each of the wagons, leaving the rest of the snow around the sides, making wind-proof dugouts. Grandfather and I shared one, and Daniel Henrie and his young wife Amanda shared the other.

I dragged along behind my grandfather as we searched for wood. We'd burned all the fuel close to the wagons days before. I was so miserable I wasn't watching where we were going nor was I looking for wood as I was supposed to. I walked with my head down and followed the fresh footprints made by my grandfather who was breaking trail ahead of me.

I did not want to get to know this gruff man who was my dead mother's father. I did not like him. He was impatient and ornery. From the little I knew about him already, I could understand why Mother and Grandmother had stayed in the east when my restless Grandfather had come west. He'd been a mountain man for awhile, then settled down to a small ranch. He kept writing to Grandmother, trying to persuade her to join him, but she never did. And then she'd died.

My father had gone to college in New York, met my mother, and married her. After I was born, we had a perfectly happy little family, until the missionaries came. My mother and father joined The Church of Jesus Christ of Latter-day Saints and headed west for Zion, for a perfect life, for peace and happiness. My mother died on the trek. That took away my happiness. If I had even had a testimony before then, it died with my mother.

I was startled out of my miserable thoughts when I bumped into the back of my grandfather. I quickly stepped back, and he threw a disgusted look over his shoulder at me. Instead of speaking, he pointed, like I was some kind of dog that couldn't understand speech. I followed the direction of his rough, bony finger and saw a fallen tree lying on the south-facing hillside of the canyon. A skiff of snow still clung to the bark, but the biggest part of the frozen white powder had been blown away by the canyon breeze and melted off by the infrequent sun. Although my grandfather considered me "citified," even I could see that the tree was dead, and I knew what finding a whole tree of dead wood meant to our small encampment. Warmth. "That looks too big for us to pull," I said doubtfully.

"Of course it's too big! We're goin' back to get the horses."

We slipped and scrambled our way back to camp faster than we'd left. This time I was glad to keep my head up and look around as we stomped and slid through the frozen landscape. The snow actually appeared smooth, clean and pristine this morning. I was glad to be alive.

Amanda Henrie looked out from under her wagon when she heard us approach. In the early morning light, the jagged pink scar on her cheek stood out like a fresh brand on cattle. She had been living in Salt Lake when her husband's feisty black stallion had reared up and struck Amanda in the face with his front hoof, even though she had been standing on the other side of the fence. The horse did not live another day, as Dan Henrie had shot it.

Amanda Henrie was on her way to Manti to visit her parents as well as to help deliver the desperately-needed supplies to the new settlement. Although she was much younger than my own mother and had no children of her own, I had secretly begun to think of her as my substitute mother.

"You two look like you just found a hot spring!" she said. We grinned at her like two schoolboys. When she turned her head the other way and the scar didn't show, she was exceptionally pretty.

"We found us some wood," said Grandfather.

"Well, that is a good thing, we could always use more wood!" she smiled.

"It's a whole tree!" I gushed, then stopped, realizing I sounded like a little boy.

"Well, you just get that tree on over here and I'll cook you some breakfast!" Amanda said, and started mixing biscuits. At least we ate well, since we had two wagonloads of supplies intended for a settlement of over two hundred people.

Dan Henrie showed up from around the back of the wagons, walking a team of horses toward us. "I heard you talking," he said. "I'll gladly give you a hand to get that tree closer to the fire."

We guided the horses to the tree, hitched them up to the trunk, and "yee-hawed" them back to the camp. The team pulled the dry wood easily along the hillside that was blown almost barren of snow. They seemed happy to exercise their legs.

As we got closer to the campsite at the bottom of the canyon, the horses began to lunge and pull through the deep, frozen snow collected in the shadowy places and tucked down out of reach of the canyon breeze. Hooves slipped, and breath blew out in clouds as the horses scrabbled for solid footing. The stiff, wide branches of the tree swept out a broad pathway in the snow as the team fought to pull it back to our shelters. An occasional sagebrush or rock poked its way up in the wake of our tree plow.

Blowing and snorting, the horses finally made it to the campsite. Dan Henrie spoke to them in soothing tones, "That's a boy, Patch, good job, good job. You did it, Major, good boy, good job." His deep voice rumbled continual praise to the two animals as he unhitched them and led them around to the back of the wagons.

It had taken us longer than we thought to accomplish our task, so we had cold biscuits for breakfast. Amanda had collected snow into a pan and boiled it into water. When she saw us approaching, she'd dropped in a handful of the strangely jointed green stems that grew wild in Utah and boiled up into "Mormon Tea." We had plenty of sugar to sweeten it. I felt much more optimistic after drinking a cup of the hot, sweet liquid.

After breakfast, we all helped clear more snow away from the pasture where the horses were digging and scraping with their hooves to find food. We uncovered some sparse brown grass and the horses eagerly bent their heads to eat.

There wasn't much to do now that we were set up with wood and the horses had been provided for the best we could. When Grandfather went off with his rifle to hunt for fresh meat, I crawled under our wagon and allowed some time to feel sorry for myself.

I wanted to go back to New York, where Father and I belonged. We could be good Latter-day Saints there. Why did we have to live in this wilderness to worship God? Lots of people in the eastern states went to church. Even as I argued with myself, I knew Father was only trying to do what was right. He said we were needed here. He said Grandfather needed us, since we were the only family he had. He said we should be good examples, so Grandfather would want to join the church. I didn't think Grandfather even wanted us around. I fell asleep wishing that my mother could come back and make everything all better.

Some time later, I heard snow crunching outside the wagon. Looking out, I saw that Grandfather was empty-handed. I crawled out of the shelter, hoping it was almost time for dinner. As I stood, I noticed a movement far down along the wide swath we'd made with our firewood tree.

"Grandfather, look!"

"Shush, Boy, are ya tryin' to scare it away?"

Stung by the rebuke, I fell silent for a few moments. Watching the halting progress of the brown object became more engrossing than my self-pity, so I spoke again, more quietly, "It doesn't look like a deer."

"How would you know what a deer looks like?" Grandfather squinted into the sights on his rifle. I suspected that his eyesight was failing him, but he didn't want to admit it.

The object moved sporadically, like it was wounded. I wondered if Grandfather had shot something earlier and wounded it, and now he could finish the job. I kept waiting for the bang. Suddenly I reached up and grabbed the rifle barrel.

"It's a man!" I yelled.

"How could it be?" Grandfather snapped, but he lowered his rifle and concentrated more intently on the staggering figure.

Daniel Henrie came up behind us and also watched the unusual progress of the man. "I think he's hurt," he said. Almost as if he'd heard the words, the figure fell into the snow and lay still. Dan started out along the tree drug path to investigate. "It's a trick!" said Grandfather. Daniel Henrie put his hand out toward Grandfather, motioning him to stay back and be still. Curious, I took a couple of steps toward the fallen man. "Get back!" Grandfather barked at me.

We watched Dan reach the dark lump in the snow, bend, then stagger upright, the man supported on his right side. As he made his way toward us, he called out for help. I hurried toward him. My grandfather said something, but I wasn't sure what he said and pretended I didn't hear. I only hesitated for a second when I saw that what Dan was struggling to support was a bloody Indian. I got on the other side of the drooping figure and put my arm around his cold, stiff buckskin clothes. Together we walked him to the fire. As we laid him down, Grandfather said, "You'd best leave him die."

"I can't do that," replied Dan.

"Might be sorry later, if he gets well."

"I'll concern myself with that later."

Amanda Henrie seemed glad of something to do besides cooking, and set about tearing bandages and boiling water to clean the deep cuts that crisscrossed the Indian's muscled legs. She also found a deep wound in his side, and some smaller cuts on his hands. The Indian was bandaged and covered with blankets. Dan Henrie forced some Mormon Tea into his mouth. Although he didn't seem to be awake, the Indian swallowed.

Dan built a lean-to shelter close to the fire out of evergreen branches. More branches were spread on the ground, then a blanket, then the Indian was laid on the make shift bed with more blankets and a fur robe on top of him. Dan said he would get up every two or three hours to stoke the fire.

Grandfather had dire predictions for me that night as we bedded down in our shelter. I tried not to listen as he mumbled about being murdered in our beds and "can't expect no honor from savages."

After a couple of days, the Indian woke up. He spoke some pidgin English, and Dan Henrie spoke some Indian words, so they were able to communicate. I was fascinated by the exchange, and listened intently when Dan told us what had been said.

The Indian's name was Tabinaw, and he'd been on a raiding party to an enemy Indian camp. He'd been wounded while fighting from astride his horse. A spear had struck him in the side, almost unseating him. He'd been able to gallop out of the camp with his fellow raiders. After a few miles he was so weak, he could no longer sit on his horse. When his fellows saw his weakened condition, they took the horse and left him behind.

"Oh, how awful!" gasped Amanda Henrie, her eyes troubled as she watched the wounded man.

Tabinaw understood, and looked at the white woman calmly. "It is our way," he answered.

Two days later, Tabinaw could get around. He saw our horses struggling for food and us struggling to feed them. He told us to get some branches down and let them chew on the bark and eat the smaller tips off the end to supplement their diet of dead, frozen grass. He showed me how to fashion a spear, although Grandfather grumbled about him having a knife within reach. He told fascinating stories about Indian life and customs. It was hard for me to understand it all, but I did my best and managed to learn a few Indian words along the way.

The days were no longer endless and empty. I got up eagerly each morning. The cold was in the back of my mind now, instead of being the main focus of my thoughts. Learning and doing things with Tabinaw kept me in good spirits.

One afternoon, I noticed dark shapes moving through the trees and brush toward our camp. I studied them for a few moments, and decided they were men on horses. We're found! We're rescued! Then I realized it was more likely to be Indians.

"Dan!" I called. Tabinaw looked up when he heard the urgency in my voice. Grandfather followed Dan out to where I stood. I pointed. Dan looked grim. "Looks like a war party."

The Indians broke out of the brush and into our tree-drug swath of scraped snow. They had weapons, and their faces were painted. They did not raise a hand or call a friendly greeting.

They advanced on us with deadly purpose.

I watched their approach with a dread fascination, conscious of my heart beating heavily against my ribs. I gave a gasp of surprise as Grandfather took hold of me and put me behind his tough and bony frame. His rifle was clutched in his hands, although it seemed small protection against the large war party.

One of the advancing Indians began whooping, and they all pushed their mounts to greater speed, raising their weapons as they drew nearer. Dan Henrie took hold of Amanda and pushed her toward the shelter, speaking rapidly and urgently. Grandfather muttered, "I knew it, I knew it."

Tabinaw stepped out in front of us and raised up his arms toward the menacing war party. They slowed, lowered their weapons, and then stopped, staring at Tabinaw with wonder. He began speaking rapidly to them in their own language. I couldn't understand any words, he spoke too fast. The war party dismounted. Tabinaw turned toward us and said, "These my friends."

Amanda hesitated at the doorway of the shelter. "The ones who left you?" she asked.

Tabinaw gave one nod of his head. "You safe. They no harm."

Dan whispered in Amanda's ear and she began preparing food for the visitors. They stood or sat around our fire and talked to Tabinaw, gesturing and laughing. I had never associated Indians and laughter in my mind. Before now, they'd seemed so serious and savage to me. Their painted faces and primitive weapons were a feast for my eyes. Grandfather stood silently beside me. The war party seemed to enjoy our food. They wanted more sugar, and took turns eating it plain.

When they were satisfied, they made preparations to leave. Tabinaw told Dan Henrie that he would go to the Manti settlement and tell them where we were and that we needed help. Tabinaw grinned at me, mounted a horse, and rode off with his tribesmen. I crawled inside my shelter to get the spear Tabinaw had helped me make. I heard my grandfather outside speaking to Dan. "I was wrong," he said simply. I had not thought my grandfather was capable of apologizing. Hearing the gruff apology that I never thought could come out of his mouth made me think that I didn't know my grandfather very well. There just might be something in him worth getting to know.

Amanda had fixed a grand dinner, and we ate with a satisfaction we hadn't felt since we'd been stranded. Help was on the way. It was only a matter of a few more days before we were rescued and could take the remaining supplies to the settlers. I imagined the people without food, feeling desperate, cold and hungry. I was bringing them food and news from Salt Lake City. I could speak a few words of the Indian language, and I knew how to make a spear. I felt a purpose to my life that hadn't been there before. I thought maybe New York didn't need me as much as Utah Territory did.

After our nightly group prayer, just before we separated to our shelters, Amanda looked me in the eyes. "It looks as though we won't be here much longer. I wanted to be sure you knew, John, that you'll always be special to me. Wherever we go, know that I'll always be there for you, thinking fondly of you, and will help if ever you need me." She pulled me into a brief, warm hug.

I felt a strange sensation as though my mother had spoken

the same words I had just heard come out of Amanda's mouth, as though they had both spoken together. I knew my mother was all right, and I knew then that I would be, too.

Daniel and Amanda Henrie became snow bound in Salt Creek Canyon east of Nephi while delivering supplies to the settlements. They found a seriously wounded Indian named Tabinaw, who was a brother to Chief Walkara. They nursed him back to health. When an Indian war party threatened them, Tabinaw stopped the attack then rejoined the Indians as they went to Manti to get help for the stranded supply wagons.

Iron Lady

"Mama! Indians! Two lady ones, and no kids!" I called out. I liked to give a lot of information, and get a lot of information, too. In her cross moments, Mama sometimes called me "Tattletale Tess." But I knew she relied on me.

The lady ones were the not such scary ones, but the men were. But they all looked strange, Indian men, women, or kids. Their skin was so dark, and even the boys had long black hair! They wore thick, stiff clothes made out of animal skin. Sometimes I saw Indians wearing cloth clothes they had gotten from the pioneers. Even then, they still walked different, still talked and looked different. It wasn't just the clothes.

Sometimes the kids didn't even wear any clothes. Big kids, almost my size, would run around naked in the summertime. Mama said it was disgraceful. I thought it was interesting. The Indians all smelled funny, too. Men, women, big or little, they smelled kind of greasy, smoky and earthy.

Mama came out just as I recognized one of the Indian ladies on the road as Anoet. "It's Anoet and another Indian lady I don't know," I said to Mama.

Anoet had been to our house before. She smiled broadly with her gap-toothed grin. "Miektagovan!" she called out her Indian greeting.

"Hello," Mama replied.

"This my da-ter, Kimeat," said Anoet. Kimeat looked down at the ground as Mama said hello. I looked at her suspiciously.

41

She was as big as Anoet, although she wasn't as wrinkled up. How could she be her daughter? Daughters were supposed to be little, and mothers were big. I looked up doubtfully at my mother as she invited them in. I thought something was fishy. Anoet didn't waste time. She said, "Kimeat need dress. You have dress?"

"I'll go see," Mama replied, and went into the next room. I stared politely, smiling, at the two visitors for a few moments. They weren't doing anything interesting, so I walked over to the kitchen table and lifted the cloth that was thrown over the big wooden bowl. I sniffed the yummy smell of rising bread dough. Even though baking day made the house hot, I loved it! Mama's bread was the best! As I poked at the springy dough with my finger, Anoet and Kimeat talked together in a mish-mash way. There were no words I could understand. It was a very boring conversation.

Mama came back with a faded blue dress folded over her arm. I recognized it as one she had worn to work in the fields last summer. Kimeat's eyes got big. She smiled for the first time. She took the dress and hugged it to her. "Toe-ak," she whispered, "Toe-ak!" I knew that meant "thank you."

"Now," Anoet turned to Mama with her big, gappy smile, "You have ham?"

"No, sorry, we're out of ham until we butcher again this fall."

Mama must be getting forgetful. I knew I wasn't! But to be respectful, I wrinkled up my forehead in a question. "Mama," I asked, "Don't we have a hambone left in the smokehouse?"

Mama smiled a very small smile, "It's just a bone, Tess. Anoet doesn't want just a bone."

" It has some ham on it," I said helpfully.

"Not much," Mama said as though her throat were getting sore. "Just enough to flavor one little batch of beans."

Anoet smiled, "It is good, I take!" she announced.

Mama gave me a look that made me feel smaller than I already was. She left and got the ham bone. When she came back and offered it to Anoet, she didn't hold it out very far. "It's just an old dried up bone with shreds on it," she said.

Anoet grabbed it eagerly and tucked it under her arm. "Toe-ak!" she said cheerfully.

Mama sighed, then smiled. "I must get back to work," she said as she pulled open the front door to let the Indian ladies out. I opened my mouth to tell them that Mama's work was baking bread, but Mama looked at me before I could say any words, and I closed my mouth.

After Mama put the bread in the oven, I saw three braves coming down the trail. They had on the strange, stiff kind of clothes. Their long black hair was shiny with grease. One of them carried a bow, with a leather skin full of arrows hanging down his back. Another one had a knife in a sheath at his waist. I did not like the look of them. "Mama! Indians! Three man ones!" I shrieked. These were a scary kind of Indian.

They stopped at our house. The one without any weapons pointed his face up and sniffed the air noisily. "Mmmmmm!" he said, rubbing his stomach. His friends laughed and rubbed their stomachs, too.

"We have bread," said the one with the knife. I wasn't sure if he was asking or telling. I sure didn't like the looks of them. I looked down the road hopefully. I would feel better if some lady Indians came along, too.

"The bread is not quite ready," Mama said. "You may come in and sit down and wait if you want to."

Mama turned to go into the house. I saw those three Indians look at each other with raised up eyebrows and grinning like the boys at church who took a frog in one of their pockets. Mama didn't see them. I knew I had to go in the house to keep an eye on them. They were up to no good, I thought.

They each sat on a chair in the kitchen side of the room by the table. They were talking the mishmash talk that I couldn't understand. I tried to make sense of it so I'd know what they were up to, but nothing sounded like anything I knew. I decided I'd better ask one of those Indian kids to teach me their language, clothes or no clothes.

Mama picked up her hot pads, opened the oven door, and bent over to check the bread. I could not believe what I saw next! The Indian with the bow leaned forward and put the tip of his bow under the back of my mother's skirt! My mouth opened and I pointed, but no sound would come out! I even tried to make my feet move, but they felt like they were stuck to the floor! That Indian started lifting the bow up. I could see my Mama's boots, and then her stockings! Those Indians were grinning like monkeys.

When Mama's skirt got up to her knees, she suddenly whirled around and conked that Indian right on top of his head with her frying pan! The other two Indians held as still as statues while he tipped over sideways and slid to the floor. I was scared that the Indian with the knife might jump up and stab my Mama. She still had hold of the frying pan, though, in both hands. "Get him out!" she yelled.

The two friends jumped up and grabbed the limp Indian by his arms and dragged him out the door. They didn't seem to care that his legs and feet were dragging and thumping down the front porch stairs.

Mama's face was red and her eyebrows were angry. My feet and mouth got unstuck and I ran toward her. "Mama?" I asked fearfully. Mama looked at me, put down her frying pan, and her forehead smoothed out. "I'm not angry at you, Tess!" She pulled me into her arms. Right then I wasn't scared of any Indians, men, ladies or naked kids. I knew I was safe.

It wasn't until almost dark that any more Indians came toward our house. There were two of them, and they approached slowly. It wasn't until they got to the porch that I recognized Anoet and Kimeat. Kimeat was wearing the blue dress and walking carefully. Anoet's eyes were big with wonder when she saw my mother. "You Iron Lady!" she announced.

Mama started to laugh. "Oh, is that what they're calling me now?" she said.

Anoet smiled a small, respectful smile. "They no bother you no more," she said. And they never did.

Indians had a real taste for pioneer bread and ham, and a curiosity about white man's clothes. An Indian man lifted the skirt of a pioneer woman with his bow while she was checking on the bread baking in her oven. She knocked him out with her frying pan, and his friends dragged him from the house. From that day on, she was known as "Iron Lady" among the Indians.

Horse Raid

Lying back against a woolly buffalo hide, I took hold of the tough deer meat venison with my teeth. It resisted until my strong jaws wrenched a piece off. Old toothless Wambayot could never do that. He could only sip the broth from a pot of boiled meat.

As I chewed, I felt proud of my new manhood, and idly wondered whether or not we'd soon need to go hunting again. I noticed some movement at the east end of camp. No one acted alarmed, so it wasn't an enemy raid. Curious, I sat up and watched the moving bodies, deciding if it was worth the effort to walk over there to see what was happening.

When I caught sight of Chief Walkara on a tall brown horse, I was on my feet and heading toward him in an instant. He was one of the six brothers that sometimes fought for control of the Ute tribes of central Utah. When he got down off his horse, his head was still above that of any Indians in our camp.

The chief received a bowl of boiled meat as he seated himself on the ground. Tribesmen gathered around him as he ate.

Finished, he tossed the bowl aside and spread his hands out to us. "My brothers," he said, "I have had a dream that there are fine horses many day's ride south, in the land called Mexico. Those who go with me will return as rich men. Who will go?"

I hesitated only a moment. The journey would go through the southern desert, where water holes could dry up. Poisonous snakes and scorpions liked to crawl into your sleeping blankets with you to feel the warmth of your skin. There were hostile tribes, and even the Mexicans would kill us if they caught us taking their horses. Horses were valuable. He who owned many horses was wealthy, and much respected.

The people who had moved into our valley and had to wear hats to keep their pale faces from turning red told us that it was not good to take horses. They called it "stealing," and said it made God angry. My people believed if you need something, you take it. If the one you took from needs it, he takes it back. My tribesman Senniga had taken an ax from a settlement. Axes were useful, much needed in our tribe. Senniga's ax was dull, and did not cut so good. He went to town, to a blacksmith, and said, "You sharpen ax."

Blacksmith say, "I can't sharpen. Is worn out. There no steel there."

Senniga say, "It all steel! Me steal it last night!"

Paleface settlers did not understand our ways. It was a fact of our life that a man without horses was nothing. A horse raid was a measure of manhood, and he who successfully took horses from another was looked upon as noble, and was respected. Owning horses made it so you could live a good life, and have many wives and children. Taking horses was good.

Walkara had been to California on a horse raid a few summers ago, and had come back with many fine horses. He and his brother Tabinaw, and all the braves who went with them, were very rich. On the way home, Walkara and Tabinaw had disagreed about which horses each one would get. They raised their voices louder and louder. Finally in his anger, Walkara pulled out his gun and shot Tabinaw's horse. Tabinaw mounted another horse and shot Walkara's horse. They kept shooting the horses the other brother mounted until they only had the horses they were riding to return home.

I knew Walkara could get many horses home, if he stayed master of his temper. I was ready to be a rich brave. All I had was a swaybacked old horse that had been taken from a wagon train in Wyoming. No one had ever tried to steal him.

When we set off for Mexico, there were almost as many of us as there are fingers on two hands. We rode many days, and crossed the Green River, the horses easily swimming the width of the mild current. We found enough water along the way for horses and men. It took many long, hot days to make it to the hills of Mexico. I was doubting Walkara's dream of fine horses as we traveled through cactus and sagebrush desert between brown hills.

The next day, we crossed between more hills and suddenly came upon a broad, green valley, dotted with many fine horses! I stopped and looked and looked. My heart flew like a bird. I had never seen so many horses in one place! Walkara had a shine in his eyes. "My dream is true!" he said.

That night when it was very dark, we rode slowly into the valley, our horses walking. When we drew close to the valley horses, our mounts made soft noises to them. The valley horses were curious, and made soft noises back. I was afraid that the horse noises would wake the Mexicans, and they would kill us. My legs wanted to kick my old horse and gallop after our new treasure, running away with them from the danger I felt all around me.

Walkara had said that moving slowly kept the new horses from being startled or running away. I held my fear inside me and kept my legs tight around the old sway back as we walked our horses into a big, curved line behind the horses in the valley. We rode slowly back toward the hills, our newly acquired wealth walking and sometimes trotting ahead of us, tossing their heads and looking back with curious eyes. We kept moving steadily toward the stars shaped like a big bear in the sky.

When we made it out of the valley and up into the hills, I turned and looked behind us. There were no lights, no sign of us being followed.

I knew that by morning, there would be armed Mexicans after us. If we were seen, we would be shot. If we were captured alive, we would probably be tortured before being killed. I had been taught to say, "It is a good day to die," when I saw that death was close at hand, but I did not want to die. I wanted to live as a rich brave, and enjoy these fine horses. My new wealth would allow me to marry some wives to take care of my teepee, and I would have many strong sons and beautiful daughters.

Walkara set a faster pace. As dawn broke, he was riding in front of the herd, letting the new horses follow his horse, as it showed them which way to go. The rest of us were riding behind to keep the horses together.

I looked back on the ground, and saw the tracks that more than two hundred horses left in the dirt, and knew that even a paleface could follow our trail. Our pursuers would not be far behind us. I imagined at any moment hearing shouts of discovery and bullets thudding into my skin. I urged my horse to go faster. We only stopped for water and ate dried venison as we rode.

When we got into familiar surroundings Walkara sent scouts to see whether the Mexicans had turned back, as he suspected they had. The scouts returned quickly, saying they were still following. Walkara picked up the pace again, and the tired horses loped along after him, heads hanging.

I did not recognize the Green River when we came to it. It was no longer a calm river. It was fast and wide. Large logs and rocks were rolling along with the strong current. The rain had fallen in the mountains while we were gone, and it had run down all the mountain gullies and valleys and gathered together in force in the river. Our tired horses refused to get in the water to swim across. Even if they had tried, in their tired state and with the fast water, they would have been swept away and drowned, or killed with the rocks and logs. I felt heavy with hopelessness, and pained with fear.

The scouts who had seen the Mexicans following us urged Walkara to abandon the horses and ride for his life. They already had their horses pointed upriver to find a narrower crossing.

Chief Walkara looked at them with a sneer. "Are you women?" he asked sarcastically. "Are you children, that you cry and run when you are scared?" I felt a pang of shame that I had thought the same thing. Walkara turned to the rest of us, pointedly ignoring the scouts. "I need some of you brave men to guard the horses, and some of you go with me to meet the Mexicans."

"But they will kill you!" said Walkara's brother, Arropine.

"They have never seen me," was Walkara's reply, "They won't know it is me." He looked at Arropine and me. "You come with me," he said. My heart felt like it would hammer out of my chest. I did not want to go back to see the Mexicans, but I did not want to tell Walkara that.

I followed his directions to cut certain horses out from the herd. They were not the best horses. Some I could tell were old, and some were not well formed. It did not take long. The horses were now used to us, and they were tired, so did not run away.

We pushed the small, scrawny horse herd ahead of us as we began back down the trail we'd just traveled. Walkara said only one thing to us, "I chose you for your closed mouths."

It didn't take us as long as I had hoped before we saw many men in large hats approaching us along the trail. They had rifles at their sides. When they spotted us, some men pulled their rifles out. I did not like the looks of this. I wished I had stayed back in camp and never gone to get horses. Better a poor man with one old horse, than a dead man in the desert. I let none of my feelings show on my face. I kept it still and straight.

Walkara raised his hand to the approaching Mexicans and called out, "There you are! I thought we'd never find you! We have had a long journey to return your horses to you!"

The Mexican in the lead, a broad faced, squinty-eyed man, said angrily, "These are not all of our horses!"

Walkara put on a sad face. "No, they aren't. Chief Walkara went crazy. He started shooting the braves who were with him. He said he wanted all the horses for himself. He even shot some of the horses! He was possessed by evil spirits! We were lucky to escape with our lives! Many of our friends are dead." If I hadn't already made my face stiff, I think my jaw would have fallen down at the story I heard Walkara tell.

Then Walkara put on a friendly face. "We brought you as many horses as we could. We did not want them in the hands of that crazy man. They should go to their rightful owners."

The Mexicans listened to what Walkara said, then talked angrily among themselves. I did not understand all of what they said. The squinty-eyed man finally turned back to us and said, "We will catch Walkara, and kill him, and get the rest of our horses back! Show us where he went, and we will avenge your friends."

Fear ran painful cactus prickles through my body. I let none of it show on my face. I kept my face still as death. If they rode ahead, they would surely find the fine horse herd by the side of the Green River, and kill us all very slowly for making fools out of them.

Walkara lowered his head and shook it side to side. "Walkara is many days ahead of you. We rode for two days to get back here. He is in the strongholds of the mountains where he lives now, and we will never catch up to him." He looked directly at the Mexican and said with such hate in his voice that even I believed he meant what he said, "Walkara is a devil! We hope to never cross his path again!"

The Mexicans spoke some more, looked over at the small herd we had brought with us, and seemed to slump in their saddles. "Alright," said the Mexican, "We thank you for the horses you brought back to us. We will rest and eat before we go home. You may eat with us."

"Thank you," said Walkara humbly.

While eating with the Mexicans, Walkara spoke again of the terror of being around evil, crazy Walkara, the sacrifice of losing his friends, and the hardship of traveling so far to bring the horses back. By the time we parted company, the Mexicans had paid him in gold coins for his trouble.

We watched them depart southward. Walkara spoke to us as they rode away, saying things like, "Now where shall we go? I don't want to go back to live with Walkara, so shall we go west? Maybe we will travel east? What do you say?"

When the Mexicans were out of sight, Walkara headed north and we rode back to the bank of the Green River. There we rested and waited until the river went down enough for the horses to cross.

We returned to our tribe in triumph. I was much admired for my strong, beautiful horses. I had been to Mexico. I had proved my bravery. Life was good.

Chief Walkara was an accomplished horse thief. He took a band of Indians to Mexico, stole hundreds of horses, and was keeping ahead of the angry owners in pursuit until his horse herd reached a flooded river. He cut the poorest horses out and took them back to meet his pursuers. He pretended to be an enemy to Walkara. The vigilantes paid him for his trouble, and returned to Mexico.

The Broken Man

"Thanks, Ma," I said as I got up from the table. My younger brothers Andrew and Erastus kept on eating.

"Do you guys have hollow legs, or are you just trying to put off your chores?" I said. They both looked at me and grinned around their mouthfuls of food.

Little Hannah, blonde and blue-eyed, looked up at me and said hopefully, "Can I come with you?"

"No, Hannah, I've got to go to work." Disappointment clouded my sister's face. I couldn't just leave her like that. Her sad eyes tugged at my heart, so I bent, gave her a hug, and said, "I'll play with you tonight after work." Hannah brightened, smiled and nodded eagerly.

We were all missing Pa, who had gone to Salt Lake City for supplies. I tried to do my best to fill in for him, to help Ma out, but my brothers didn't always think they had to mind me. I looked forward to Pa being back within the week.

Stepping out into the brisk autumn morning, I paused to admire the tall mountains speckled with bright yellow aspens and flaming red maples. Starting down the road at a brisk walk, I checked my pockets to be sure that the thick gloves needed for work were there. The thought of handling timber without their protection was a painful one. Slivers, torn skin, and bleeding blisters were all possible consequences. Little did I know that by the end of the day, those injuries would be counted as nothing.

I was fifteen and strong from working lumber with Brother Mickel all summer. We had recently been sawing logs into boards. It was a difficult process that required coordination and precision. I hoped that by now we had sawn enough boards so I could make a delivery. I was ready to do something different.

The San Pitch valley was growing in population, and lumber was needed for building projects. I was most curious about the talk of a temple that was supposed to be built on a hill in Manti that Brigham Young had dedicated. So far nothing had been done on the building. I wondered if it would be built after the style of the Nauvoo temple.

"Hello, Lewis!" Brother Mickel greeted me. A large red-faced man with a perpetual smile on his face, my employer already had the wagon in position, the pile of rough-sawn lumber that we had been working on rising behind it like a miniature mountain.

"Are you feeling strong today?" Brother Mickel asked.

"As a bear," I answered. I pulled on my gloves and positioned myself at the opposite end of the lumber stack from my employer. Working together in practiced rhythm, it wasn't long before we had the wagon piled high with the fragrant wood. As I tied the load down with rope, Brother Mickel hitched up the horses. I had driven these horses before, and they were a good team.

"If you get back in time, we'll load up one more for tomorrow," Brother Mickel said with a smile.

"I'll be sure to drive slowly," I answered. I heard Brother Mickel chuckling to himself just before I slapped the reins on the horses to get them moving.

We rolled along uneventfully for a couple of miles, and then

I topped a rise on the dirt road and started down the other side. To help the horses keep ahead of the wagon that was now propelling itself down the hill, I pushed on the brake. The wagon did not slow down. I pushed harder. There was a skiffing sound, and a screech. I felt the brake trying to grab the wheel.

"C'mon, c'mon," I muttered as the wagon crowded the trotting team. The horses were tossing their heads high, turning their eyes back for quick, worried glances at the wagon that was fast on their heels. I pushed the brake with all my might, but it wasn't enough. The wagon bucked a little, as if trying to comply with my demand, but the brake must have been worn out. It wouldn't slow the wagon down, even when I stood up and put my full weight on it.

I'll never know if it would have been better for me to have been sitting down when the traces broke. The wagon tongue suddenly fell as the connection to the horses snapped. It jammed into the road, acting as a brake which abruptly brought the wagon up short. The sudden, unexpected halt made me lose my balance and fall forward. The reins fell from my hands as I spread them to try to save myself. There was nothing I could do to stop my fall. One minute I was standing on top of the wagon, the next, I was falling. There was nothing to hold onto, nothing to grab to keep myself from hitting hard onto the dirt-packed road. I landed with a bone-cracking jolt that forced the air out of my lungs.

That would have been bad enough, but my ordeal was not yet over. The jolt that forced the wagon to a sudden stop only served to channel the forward momentum into a rolling tumble that flipped the wagon over. The heavy load I had tied down so securely just a short time ago snapped the ropes as easily as if it was thread. Before I could catch my breath and make any effort to escape, I realized with a sense of horror that I was being buried under an avalanche of wood. Like a terrifying nightmare that I couldn't wake up from, I felt the heavy timbers pelt me mercilessly, punishing my body, bruising me, crushing me, burying me alive.

I don't know how long I lay there. I felt like I was in a hazy fog. Sound and motion seemed to come from a long distance away. I felt the weight lifted off my face. I knew it was my face, but it didn't seem like it was still attached to my body. I could feel the sun on my cheek, but my eyes wouldn't open. A faraway voice was calling, sobbing, "Lewis!" It sounded like Brother Mickel. I felt bad that he was so worried. I didn't want him to be upset, so I tried to tell him I was sorry about the wagon. I tried to explain about the worn brake, but my mouth wouldn't move. Why couldn't I move? It felt like my body was as stiff and unresponsive as the wood that had buried me. Then, without warning, such an intense pain ripped through my being that when it reached my head, I mercifully blacked out.

When I woke up, instead of a dusty road under me and a heavy pile of lumber on top of me, I was lying on a real bed with a blanket for a covering. Had I dreamed the horrible accident? My eyes opened and recognized my house. My head hurt. I tried to raise my hand to explore the sore spot. My right arm wouldn't move. Panicked, I looked down and saw a large splint of boards fastened securely to my right arm, making it look like a huge homely rag doll. I raised my left arm, which moved according to my command, but it felt tender, sore and bruised. The motion caused an agony of sensation that shot so sharply through my chest and stomach that I cried out.

My mother appeared at the side of the bed, her bright smile warm and soothing in spite of the tears I could see in her eyes. Beside her was Doctor Jacobs. I could see the faces of Andrew and Erastus staring solemnly at me.

"Is he dead?" Hannah asked, her little face as grave as a mourner's.

"No, of course not," Ma said in a falsely bright voice. "See? He blinked his eyes."

"Can he play with me now?" Hannah asked hopefully.

"No, Sweetheart, he got hurt. You go play with Andrew and Erastus."

"I want to play with Lewis."

"Later. Run along," Ma said, "Lewis needs to sleep so he can get better." The children reluctantly left the room.

I made several attempts before I could get any sound out of my mouth. "Ma," I said, and the effort of speaking caused pain to jab through my jaw and neck. "What happened?"

Ma sat on a chair that was beside the bed. She took my left hand in hers and held it gently. "You had an accident, Lewis. Mr. Mickel knew something was wrong when he saw his team of horses heading back to his place, dragging their broken traces. So he went down the road and found you. He brought you here." Her voice broke, "He thought you were dead."

"I don't remember," I said drowsily, then closed my eyes against the pain that seemed to be invading every corner of my body. "What's wrong with my arm?"

Dr. Jacobs answered me. "It's broken. Your leg is also broken, in at least two places. You broke your collarbone, too."

I swallowed and my throat hurt. "Inside hurts real bad."

"Well, Son, that load of lumber was heavy. To put it bluntly, you're pretty mashed up inside. I've done all I can for you now. I'll check back tomorrow."

As he turned to leave, a tear squeezed out the corner of my eye. I hurt so much. My mother laid my hand down gently. "I'll get you some broth I steeped with willow bark for the pain."

After I took a few mouthfuls of the weak broth, I fell asleep again. It was just too much work to swallow.

Brother Mickel's stern voice woke me up. "Lewis Anderson!" I opened my eyes and stared with consternation at the unsmiling face of Brother Mickel. I had never seen him look so serious.

"Of all the ways to get out of working, I've never known a man to play dead before!" Then he smiled.

I swallowed carefully, exploring the pain level. I tried to smile back, but it didn't work. "Honestly, sometimes it hurts so bad I wish I was dead," I murmured.

"Would you like a blessing?" Brother Mickel said.

"Yes." I didn't nod my head because it would hurt too much.

Dr. Jacobs was there, checking up on me again. He assisted Brother Mickel. They laid their hands gently on my head, taking care not to touch the wounds that were bandaged. A calmness and comfort coursed through me, and I relaxed and fell asleep before they finished.

When Pa got home, I felt ashamed that I still couldn't get up, even to use the outhouse. I knew Pa needed me, that he depended on me to help him in this new land that we were settling. Pa was upset, but it wasn't at me. He was upset that the accident had happened at all. He gave me a blessing, too.

I watched my family struggle to prepare for winter. On more than one occasion I heard someone chopping wood

60

outside and longed to go out and take over for them, to feel the axe handle in my hands, my two strong arms hefting it up, then swinging it down with a satisfying "crack," splitting the firewood with one chop. I imagined my two whole legs, muscled and unbroken, bending to get an armful of the split wood. Then I would walk it over to the woodpile by the house for Ma to use in cooking. I had never before appreciated the blessing of a strong, healthy body.

By the time the snow was deep and the bitter cold winter had set in, Doctor Jacobs pronounced my bones healed and took off the splints. When I tried to get up to test my legs, intense pain tore through my insides. I fell back onto the bed, disgusted and disappointed, tears of frustration running into my ears.

Although they never complained, I felt like a terrible burden to my family. I ate the food that they had harvested and stored, wore the clothes that Ma mended and washed for me, and laid in the biggest bed in the house. I wasn't doing anything useful or contributing to the family upkeep. My loved ones might be better off if I had died. Then at least there would be one less mouth to feed, and they'd have more room in the house for the members of the family that were doing their share to earn their food and sleeping space.

I forced myself to stand a little bit every day. The bones had healed, but in my opinion I wasn't getting well fast enough.

As the winter wore on, cold and chill, my heart began to feel shrunken and hard, like a chunk of ice. I began to hope that if Father in Heaven wasn't going to heal me, he would take me home to Him and bless my family with the release of my burdensome care.

The winter was dragging on, reluctant to let go of its icy hold on the world. I ate as little as I possibly could, and spent most of my time sleeping or staring out the window. I felt so bad about myself I didn't want to play with Andrew or Erastus or even Hannah, who puckered up her face with worry whenever I caught her looking at me. I didn't want to listen to Ma read to me or have Pa play his mouth organ. It was just no good.

My family usually left when I wouldn't respond to their entreaties to do something cheery, telling themselves I must just be tired, that was all. Thus I was alone one soggy spring day, staring out the window at the dirty piles of snow that were melting into mud.

My habitual dour thoughts were chasing each other around in my head like flies buzzing around a rotten carcass, when they suddenly stopped short. I stared at the window, my mouth dropping open in amazement. Where I had just been gazing at the puny struggle that spring was making to come to the valley, I now saw a beautiful white building, with arched windows and two towers, the whole edifice shining steadily before my eyes as though cupped reverently in some invisible, eternal hands. My whole body felt warm and light, the darkness of my mind lifting at the beautiful sight. My heart began to pound with joy and a zest for living that had been sorely lacking for a long time. I gazed at the radiant building until my heart was full of it, until it was impressed on my mind and had filled my soul with hope and wonder. Then it gradually faded away.

After that glorious experience, it seemed as though my body recovered at a much faster rate. I began to focus on things I could do instead of what I couldn't. By the time new grass was forcing its way up through the thick brown mud, I was walking with a cane, Hannah keeping a close vigil at my side, matching her little feet to my halting steps, smiling up at me and telling me what a good boy I was. I insisted on hauling water whenever

I could get to the bucket before Andrew. I challenged Erastus to race to the woodpile, his face beaming as he handily beat his big brother. My mother cautioned me. My father encouraged me. Brother Mickel confided to me that Doctor Jacobs had told my mother the first day he examined me that I would probably be dead the next day. "It's a good thing he set your bones straight anyway!" Brother Mickel laughed.

Ironically, I stayed in the lumber industry and was called a few years after my accident to work at the temple sawmill in Canal Creek Canyon above Spring City. I worked with Bishop Amasa Tucker as he oversaw the selection of lumber for use in building the temple at Manti. Although I never actually visited the building site, I did deliver lumber out of the canyon periodically. It became a firm habit to check the brakes on any wagon before driving it.

The temple was still four years away from being completed when I was called on consecutive missions to Wisconsin, Minnesota, and Illinois.

Upon my return home, I was pleased to be called as temple recorder. I eagerly traveled to Manti for the temple dedication and my first look at the new House of the Lord. As the magnificent building came into view, my breath caught in wonder. Staring at the Manti Temple, I recognized it as the building I had seen in the vision that pulled me out of my deep depression years before. My eyes filled with tears as warmth filled my body. "There is the building I saw as a boy," I whispered.

The temple continued to be a significant part of my life, and thirty eight years later I was called as the temple president. I served gladly until the end of my days, which was twenty seven more years, in the sacred building that brought such meaning and joy to my earthly existence. I really was home.

Lewis Anderson was crushed under a load of lumber when the brakes on the wagon he was driving failed. He was presumed dead. He became despondent during his long recovery, until one day he saw a vision of the temple. When he recovered, he helped cut lumber for the temple, but never saw the building until he returned from his lengthy proselyting mission. When he saw the Manti Temple for the first time, he recognized it as the building from his vision. He served as temple president from 1906 until his death in 1933.

Hostage Baby

"Simeon, you're choking me!" I coughed, crawling on my hands and knees as my two-year-old cousin grabbed my neck to keep from sliding off my back. Either I wasn't a very good horsey or he wasn't a very good rider.

Aunt Hannah came in and plucked Simeon off of me. "What are you doing to Matthew?" she scolded him gently.

"Aw, it's all right," I mumbled as I stood up, accidentally kicking a corner of the braided rug into a big fold. As I hurried to smooth it, I said, "He was just playing with me. It's too cold and wet to play outside. I'm sorry if we disturbed you." I was disappointed that my apology didn't keep Aunt Hannah from carrying Simeon into the kitchen with her. His big blue eyes stared at me over her shoulder until he disappeared into the other room. I had done it again! Even when I apologized and tried to make it right, everything went wrong!

It was all Dan's fault. I hadn't wanted Ma to go and marry Dan, but she had anyway. If that wasn't bad enough, she went and had Aaron! A messy, smelly, noisy baby who got her attention every time he bawled. I hated my life. It had been much better before Dan and Aaron came; even with Pa dead, it was better than it was now.

I had decided to confront Ma when Dan was nowhere in sight. She had been in the parlor, holding her new baby, as usual. I went in and sat by her. "Ma, are you happy?"

"Why, yes, Matthew, most of the time." She smiled at me absently, "Are you?"

"No!" I blurted, surprising myself when I felt all my resentment spilling out of my mouth like a burst dam. "Why'd you have to go and marry Dan? He's not anything like Pa! And why'd you have Aaron?" Ma instinctively tightened her hold on the infant. That just added fuel to the fire I felt inside me. I plowed on, unable to stop myself, "What do you need me for? You have another husband, another son! I'm just in the way. I should die like Pa!"

Ma looked as though I had struck her. "Matthew!" Dan snapped at me from the doorway, "Don't talk to your mother that way!"

I turned on him. "She's my mother, you can't tell me how to talk to her, because you're not my father!" I yelled. Dan's face went red, and I thought he might try to grab me, so I ran outside. The sound of my mother's crying ripped at my heart as I ran. I hated Dan. I wished with all my might that he would go back where he came from and leave us alone. I decided I hated Pa, too. Why did he go and die on us? He made this problem! And Ma. She could have left well enough alone! Why didn't she love me anymore? I felt guilty about hurting her feelings. I felt mean. I knew Pa would have been terribly disappointed in me.

I roughly wiped the tears that I didn't remember crying off my face. I wasn't going to cry like a baby. I walked and walked and walked. I finally decided if Ma didn't need me, I didn't need her. I whirled and stalked toward home. On the way, I decided that, just for good measure, I hated babies, too, and would stay as far away from them as I could. The closer I got to home, the colder my heart felt.

Ma greeted me calmly, " Matthew, sit down." Dan and Aaron were nowhere in sight. My heart jolted with hope as the sudden thought crossed my mind that Ma had sent them away for good. "You know I love you very much," she continued as she touched my arm. My mean resolve started to melt. I opened my mouth, but she put up her hand. "Let me finish, my dear. Since I love you so much, I'm concerned that you seem very unhappy here. I think you should go to Manti and visit my sister Hannah. Come back for planting. We'll need you, and I'll be missing you so desperately, you'll have to come home anyway." Ma smiled hopefully at me. I made my face hard, like my heart. Ma continued, "It would be an adventure for you! Matthew, I think it's for the best, so I want you to go."

Then Ma reached over and hugged me. I didn't want her to let go. I couldn't look at her. She said she loved me, but she was sending me away.

I felt like I was made of wood as I prepared to leave. It hurt inside when I left my mother behind in Salt Lake City, but I squashed the hurt with the hardness.

Now I was in Manti, with Aunt Hannah, who wasn't much like my mother. She was so proper I didn't know how to act around her. It didn't help that my arms and legs were growing faster than I could keep up with them. I felt clumsy even when I was sitting still. One good thing about being here was that Uncle Isaac Morley was famous in Manti. Being his nephew made me feel kind of famous, too. I admired how he could be tough, but kind. He was fair. He was the one Brigham Young appointed to lead the settlers to Sanpete in 1849.

After my resentment at being here had worn off some, I had to admit it was kind of exciting, living so close to Indians. We had Indians come into Salt Lake City, but they came into town. Here, they were so close, it was almost like living with them. I had even seen their camps of teepees, dogs, cooking fires, and hanging fleshed hides.

Besides the Indians, I had found a friend in Jim, who was a few years older than me. He was still unmarried, so he still knew how to have fun. I had gone out with him one evening and he'd pulled a long piece of twine from his pocket. When he produced a large nail and grinned at me, I was baffled. He tied the nail to the end of the twine, shushed me, and led the way over to the woodpile at Anderson's house.

Jim threw the twine over the roof and we bent down behind the pile of wood. When Jim gave the twine several gentle tugs, I heard a faint "tick-tick-tick" from the other side of the house. Next I heard movement and voices from inside. After a few more minutes of Jim tapping the nail against the window, Brother Anderson appeared from around the corner of the house and ran on past us, his white nightshirt flapping in the moonlight, his breath making little clouds in the nippy air every time he exhaled.

We could hear childish laughter coming from inside the house. I felt a tug of jealousy as I imagined those little Anderson kids watching their Pa run around the house in his nightshirt, delighting in his strength and trusting him to protect them from whatever was making that tick-tick-ticking noise.

It ended up that Brother Anderson found the nail, and pulled on the string so hard that it yanked right out of Jim's hand. We burst out of the woodpile and ran off into the darkness, followed by Brother Shoemaker's good-natured yell, "Go home and get some sleep, you scalawags!"

If it hadn't been for Jim and the Indians, Manti would have been too boring to tolerate. Well, Jim, the Indians, and my baby cousin Simeon. It surprised me to admit that I really was fond of the little boy.

I turned as I heard a commotion and a babble of voices

outside. I opened the door. The freezing cold hail and sleet from earlier that day had melted into a slushy, muddy street. Two men on horses were arguing with four or five men on the ground. Uncle Isaac approached the group.

"Shut the door, Matthew, it's cold out there," Aunt Hannah said. I hadn't heard her walk up behind me. Quickly I shut the door on my foot. It bounced open and hit the wall. Flustered, I caught it again and shut it more slowly, fumbling with the latch. Aunt Hannah turned and went back into the kitchen.

My face hot with embarrassment, I looked out the window at the scene in the street. Uncle Isaac's posture was droopy. He was listening to the men on the horses, and then he shook his head sadly. He put his hand up as if to ward off any further words. He headed toward me, the mud oozing up around his boots with every step. He opened the door, and sat down to take off his boots. I was anxious to find out what had happened, but I didn't want to sound overly eager. I stood silently waiting. When Uncle Isaac looked up and saw me, his face brightened. "Hello, Matthew," he said warmly.

I wouldn't admit it to anyone, but I was secretly ashamed that after five years I couldn't recall the details of my father's face. I did remember his smile, though. I remembered the way he said my name. I figured that Uncle Isaac was about the next best thing to my own father. At least I felt like he wanted me here. When he headed for the kitchen, I followed.

"There's Papa!" Aunt Hannah said, smiling, as she handed little Simeon to Uncle Isaac. When she saw his expression, her smile disappeared. "What's wrong?" she asked.

Uncle Isaac sank down wearily into a chair. He held Simeon to his chest. "Those two new settlers, the ones from back east." Simeon squirmed to get down. Uncle Isaac kissed his son, set him on his two sturdy legs, and managed one pat on the curly blonde head just before Simeon ran away.

"What about them?" asked Aunt Hannah impatiently, scooping flour into the bowl she was mixing batter in. She stirred vigorously.

"They were up in the mountains to cut wood this morning. The hailstorm came up unexpectedly. They went to the lean-to cabin in North Fork for shelter. There were two young Indian boys in there, already taking shelter." Uncle Isaac sounded like he couldn't believe what he was saying. "They used whips and drove those two Indian boys out into the freezing sleet and hail. They beat them, and left them." He stared down at the floor, his face a mask of sorrow.

Aunt Hannah stood still. "Oh, those poor boys. Are they...?"

"I don't know if they survived," Uncle Isaac said. "I don't know." By the sound of his voice, I guessed that he feared they had not.

The next morning, when word came to our house that an Indian was approaching, Uncle Isaac registered no surprise. He stood, put on his coat and walked out into the street. The cold night had frozen the muddy street into hard lumps. I leaned over the windowsill to see who was coming. I knew some of the Indians by sight.

In my eagerness, I bumped into Aunt Hannah's favorite black vase with little pink roses painted on it. It had been her grandmother's, and survived the trip from England. As it tipped, I strained to catch it, but it slipped through my fingers. All those years and perilous travels it had been kept safe, and now it was in danger because of one clumsy boy. I was relieved to see that my effort to catch it did manage to slow its fall.

After it clattered to the floor, I picked it up and examined it anxiously. I could only find a small chip off one edge of the rim. It was hardly noticeable.

I set it back with the chipped part toward the wall and hung onto it with one hand as I looked outside again. I recognized Chief Sowiett on a paint horse making his way down the lumpy dirt street. His face was as still as an old oak tree trunk.

He dismounted slowly and came into our house. "Please, Chief, sit down," Aunt Hannah offered him a chair. He sat down awkwardly, then fixed his eyes on little Simeon in Aunt Hannah's arms. Aunt Hannah seemed nervous. "Let me go get you some bread and milk," she offered, and hurried out to the kitchen.

Uncle Isaac smiled pleasantly at the chief and spoke some words I couldn't understand. Chief Sowiett gave a long answer back. As he spoke, Uncle Isaac's smile faded and his face became grave. He shook his head sadly, then put his hand up to his eyes. Sowiett reached forward and touched Uncle Isaac's arm, speaking earnestly. Uncle Isaac nodded and managed a weak smile. I was almost wriggling out of my chair. What was going on? What were they saying? What had happened? A guy needs to know things.

Aunt Hannah brought out a bowl filled with chunks of homemade bread with milk poured over it. On the top was a drizzle of molasses. She handed it to Chief Sowiett with a spoon. He smiled in gratitude, and began to eat. He held the spoon awkwardly. It looked like he had to concentrate to balance the bread on his spoon to get it from the bowl to his mouth.

I watched intently as he took the first bite. My stomach growled loudly, and I quickly crossed my arms and pressed them into my mid-section. My mouth was watering, and I wondered if there was any more bread and milk in the kitchen.

"Excuse me, Chief Sowiett," said Uncle Isaac in English. The chief nodded and continued eating.

I followed Uncle Isaac and Aunt Hannah out to the kitchen. I sliced some bread as I listened.

"It's bad," said Uncle Isaac solemnly. "One of those Indian boys from yesterday was Chief Sowiett's son. The chief says he was about twelve winters, so he was twelve years old. He and his friend died in the night."

Aunt Hannah put her hand to her mouth and her eyes filled with tears. "What will we do? And what will he do?" She sounded both sorry and afraid. I dripped some molasses on the floor. "Chief Sowiett is sad, he says his spirit within him is wounded, but he will not exact revenge. He is a peaceful person. He does not fault our settlement for the actions of those two men."

"Thank the Lord," Aunt Hannah sighed.

We all walked back to the parlor. Chief Sowiett was gone. His bowl and spoon were placed neatly on his chair.

Later that afternoon, the message again came that Indians were approaching the settlement. Uncle Isaac looked surprised, then concerned, and again went out into the street to meet them. Approaching this time was Chief Walkara, Sowiett's brother. He was taller than Sowiett, and younger. He had other braves with him. He looked down at Uncle Isaac from astride his horse. He began speaking in loud, angry phrases, again in that language I couldn't understand. It was driving me crazy! I was going to have to learn this Indian language so I could know what was going on!

Now Uncle Isaac was speaking earnestly to Chief Walkara, putting his hands up toward him in a pleading gesture. Chief Walkara pointed toward Uncle Isaac's house, and Uncle Isaac's head sunk down on his chest.

Will Potter, an old Mormon mountain man who told the best stories I ever heard, came from out of the small crowd of people assembled to watch the drama. He spoke loud, urgent words to the chief, gesturing toward the Morley house, and then pointing to himself. Chief Walkara shook his head. Potter spoke more loudly, his words running together. Chief Walkara shook his head again and got down off his horse, heading toward the Morley's. Uncle Isaac walked ahead of him, and called to Aunt Hannah from the doorway. She came into view, holding little Simeon, her face a question. Uncle Isaac spoke urgently to her, then took hold of Simeon and pulled him from Aunt Hannah's arms. She let out a wail as Uncle Isaac handed my nephew to Chief Walkara! I could not believe my eyes!

Chief Walkara's expression was savage satisfaction as he carried the pale, blonde, whimpering baby against his dark chest. He handed the boy to one of his braves, then mounted his horse, reached out, and took Simeon back. Simeon seemed fascinated by the horse's mane, and stretched out his fat little hand to grab it as Chief Walkara turned his horse and rode out of Manti.

Heartbreaking wails reverberated through the street. They could have been coming from my own heart. Simeon was gone. I couldn't believe what I had seen. My Uncle Isaac had given his son to the savage Indians. It was as though my uncle had suddenly turned into a heartless beast! How could I ever have thought he was anything like my father? He wasn't! He wasn't even like a human being! My eyes were hot, my breath was fast, my body was aching. I felt shaky. I felt confused. I was angry, and I was scared.

I stumbled to the barn and curled up in a corner. I could still hear intermittent wails coming through the walls of the Morley house. As soon as Uncle Isaac had callously handed his son over to the chief, he had pulled my hysterical aunt inside. She hadn't watched her son ride away. But the impossible image was burned forever into my mind. Every time it re-rolled across my memory, I shuddered with fresh horror. I cried so hard, I felt like a baby myself. But I didn't care.

I decided to run away back to Salt Lake City the next morning. I would leave before anyone saw me and could try to stop me. I couldn't stay with a man who acted more savage than the Indians!

I woke up in the dark. I was cold inside and out, but made my way to the now silent house. I slipped inside the back door and stepped quietly and carefully along the rough wooden floorboards. Heading for the loft, my head turned involuntarily toward a disturbing glow in the parlor that faintly illuminated the kitchen, like ghost light. I saw Aunt Hannah kneeling beside a chair in the light of an oil lamp. She was talking, but I knew it was not to herself. She was praying. I crawled silently into my small, cold bed.

I slept late the next day. No one woke me up to help with chores. There were no smells of food cooking. The house was too quiet. Since people were already up and moving about, I re-thought my plan and decided to leave late that night. I didn't want anyone to stop me. I didn't want to have to try to explain. Even the thought of speaking my feelings closed my throat up tight.

I felt restless. I caught myself looking for Simeon to tickle, and throw up into the air. When I remembered, I felt a sharp pain clear into my soul. It scared me to realize how much I loved my little cousin.

I couldn't stand being in the house any more. I escaped outside so I wouldn't be surrounded and suffocated by memories of Simeon and the sorrow of my own heart. "Hey, Matthew," called Jim.

"Hey," I replied without looking up.

"What do you think about that Will Potter? That was sure something when he talked to Walkara yesterday!"

It felt like something broke inside of me, and anger spilled out. "I don't think anything," I shouted, "I don't know what anyone said, and I don't know why Uncle Isaac gave Simeon away! And to savages! He didn't fight for his own son! He didn't even try! He just gave him away! How could he do that? How could he do something as cruel as that?" I swiped at my eyes angrily. Jim put his hand on my back.

"I didn't know you hadn't heard," he said gently. "Walkara came to demand satisfaction for his nephew being killed."

"That's stupid!" I yelled, "Chief Sowiett didn't want any kind of revenge, and it was his son that was killed! Not Walkara's!"

"True. But Walkara still demanded satisfaction for his sorrow, for the loss of his nephew. He demanded blankets, flour, and sugar. We don't have as much as he wanted. Father Morley told him he'd have to send to Salt Lake City for the supplies.

Walkara said that to ensure his ransom would be delivered, he wanted Father Morley's son as hostage. Father Morley pleaded, but Walkara's heart is hard as stone. Then, what Will Potter was telling Walkara, was that if he would take him in the child's place, he would be Walkara's slave! He said the baby couldn't work, or be any help to the great chief. Walkara refused. Father Morley knows that there are more Indians than us. The entire settlement was in danger. If Walkara was offended and declared war, Simeon could be killed anyway. So

75

all he could do was give the boy up and trust in God."

"What kind of God?" I said bitterly, feeling shocked inside myself as the words came out of my mouth. I thought Jim would turn away and call me a blasphemer. Instead, he slid his arm over my shoulder and tightened it into a hug. I felt my hard heart soften. A silent cry rose inside my soul for God to please watch over that curly haired baby that liked to about choke me to death! I let out a loud sob, and, embarrassed that Jim had heard me, headed back to the Morley house. Jim watched me trip and almost fall, but he didn't approach me or follow me.

At the Morley house, no one smiled. No one spoke, except Aunt Hannah, to pray. No food was fixed—not that I wanted any. Everything was so unnatural and depressed so that I felt like I was sitting inside a grave.

About an hour before dark, a great shout went up in the street. My heart constricted. What now? I didn't want any more adventures of any kind. I just wanted to go home to my mother.

There was a pounding on the door. My aunt stared at it, white-faced. It was Uncle Isaac who opened it. A man I didn't know very well stood in the doorway, his face red, his eyes wide. "He's coming!" he yelled.

Uncle Isaac stepped outside. Aunt Hannah put her hand to her throat and followed him. I was right behind her, and accidentally stepped on her dress, but she didn't seem to notice. Her eyes were focused on the little procession that was coming down the street. When I saw what was approaching, my mouth fell open. I could have fit a whole wagonload of hogs into it.

The Indians from the day before were back, tall Chief Walkara riding proudly behind a little white pony with blonde Simeon Morley sitting on it. He was dressed in a miniature set of Indian buckskins, and his skin was brown. I later learned that walnut juice had been rubbed on his skin to stain it. His round blue eyes caught sight of his parents and he burst into smiles. "Mama!" he called. I don't think even a grizzly bear could have stopped Aunt Hannah. She gave a strangled sound and ran to meet her baby son, snatched him off the horse, and raced for the house. After she slammed the door, I heard the click of the bolt sliding into place.

Chief Walkara wore a smug look on his dark features. Uncle Isaac said something to him. His voice broke. Chief Walkara replied in a stately voice. Uncle Isaac put his hand out toward the chief, who still sat astride his horse. Chief Walkara took it stiffly. I could tell he wasn't used to shaking hands. After the white man's handshake, the chief raised his hand to Uncle Isaac, palm forward, then turned his horse and led his entourage back to the Indian camp, leaving the little white horse behind. I was all smiles. "Jim! Jim! Tell me what happened!" Jim was smiling, too. Every face I saw was smiling. The whole world was smiling.

"He told your uncle that since he had trusted Chief Walkara with his own son, the chief knew that he could trust Father Morley to deliver the blankets and flour and sugar. He said he didn't need to keep Simeon any more, he knew 'Chief Morley' would keep his word."

"Thanks, Jim!" I said, as though he had personally delivered Simeon back to the settlement. He grinned at me. It felt like the hard, icy lump inside me had melted down to my toes. I felt warmth and respect for Uncle Isaac instead of the intense anger and hate I had felt for him earlier. A prayer of thankfulness welled up in my heart and burst out of my mouth in a quiet "thank you!" which I imagined floating up to the Heavens.

I longed to see my mother. I was ready to go back to Salt Lake City, apologize to her with all my soul, and make friends with my own baby brother.

In my joyous, soft hearted state, I could even admit that I hadn't been fair to Dan. I'd never tried to get to know him. I knew he never would replace my father, but that didn't mean we couldn't get along. Maybe I would be a man, take the first step, and break the ice. After all, I had a whopper of a story to tell!

Chief Sowiette's son was killed by white men. He wanted no revenge. Chief Walker demanded payment of goods, and took 2-year-old Simeon Morley from his father Isaac as hostage until the goods were delivered. Will Potter offered to go in the baby's place. Hannah prayed all night long. Simeon was returned the next day on his own pony with his own set of buckskins and his skin dyed brown.

Killer In The Henhouse

I didn't mean to kill the chicken. Honest. I only threw my corncob to the hens because they like to peck on them even after all the kernels are eaten off. After dinner it was almost all dark, so I threw it as hard as I could to be sure to get it over the fence. One of the hens said, "BA-KAW!" so loud and cheerful, I said, "You're welcome!" as I walked back to my house.

The next morning I answered a knock on the door. Our neighbor, Addie, was standing there. She was as old as my granny, with whom I lived because I didn't have a mother or father alive. In one hand Addie dangled a dead chicken upside down by the feet. In her other hand she held an empty corncob. I put my hands on my hips like I'd seen my Granny do. "What on earth happened to your chicken?" I asked.

"That's what I was going to ask you!" Addie said to me. Then something clicked in my head, like maybe I was in trouble, and a cold shiver ran down my backbone. I do not ever, ever like to be in trouble. I pulled my bottom lip down, then asked casually, "Is that my corncob, or yours?"

"It's not mine."

Granny came over to see who I was talking to. "Come in, Adelia!" she said, then frowned. "What on earth happened to your chicken?"

I had been studying the stiffened bird and wondering, when a sudden thought struck me. It knocked the shivery feeling clear into yesterday! This was a matter of life or death! "Was the corn poison?" I asked in horror, covering my mouth and feeling my stomach lurch.

"No. Near as I can tell, this corncob bonked this chicken on the head. It hit so hard, it killed her."

My mouth fell open. I, Cissy Sorenson, threw a corncob hard enough to kill a chicken? Wow! My heart got all warm and big in my chest. I was stronger than I thought! I rolled my shoulders experimentally inside my long sleeved gingham dress. Yes, the sleeves felt tighter than yesterday. I squeezed my arm muscles with my fingers. They felt small, but tough.

Just wait until I saw that Jacob Olsen again! Just see if he thought he could push me around anymore! I'd show him a thing or two! I got a little grin on my face thinking of what I could do to Jacob now that I was strong enough to kill a chicken with one throw!

Granny looked sharply at me. "Cecelia!" she said in a warning tone of voice. I stared up at the two big ladies. It wasn't fair that grown ups were so much bigger than kids. How would they like it if kids were bigger than them?

I switched my gaze to the slightly flattened, stiff bird in Addie's hand so I wouldn't have to look at her angry eyes, then put on my stubborn mouth so I wouldn't cry. I would never do anything mean to Addie. Even though she was old, she was my friend—or she used to be. Before the chicken. I glared at the dead hen. Stupid bird couldn't even dodge a corncob.

Addie and I both liked chickens. Her henhouse was between our houses, and I liked to watch the busy way the hens cluck-clucked to each other, scratching in the dirt and pecking on the ground. They were especially funny to watch when they chased a bug! Sometimes two of them would both get hold of a grasshopper at the same time. Then they would have a tug of war! Sometimes they'd pull the grasshopper in half!

"CECELIA!"

I jumped. In spite of my stubborn mouth, my chin quivered. "I was just feeding the chickens! I didn't mean to! I'm sorry, sorry, sorry! I'll never eat corn again!" I swiped my eyes angrily with my sleeve. I'd run away. I'd go into the mountains and live with the Indians. They didn't have any chickens.

"Cissy," Addie said in a soft voice. I looked up at her warily. Cissy is my name when I'm being good. "You may feed my chickens any time you want to. I only ask two things."

"What?" I said suspiciously.

"First, feed them more gently." Addie smiled, "And next time you kill one, do it in the daytime so we can eat it before it spoils!"

"Deal!" I said, and held out my hand to shake Addie's, but hers were still full of chicken and corn.

I watched her head for her house. Even though we lived next door, her house was about a block away.

Later that day, Granny made me go out to pick some squishy ughy squash, which is only good if it's in a pie. I saw Addie come out in her yellow apron. She wore it almost all the time. I'd first seen it as an armful of yellow cloth that spring when Addie came over to complain to Granny.

"I got this to make some pants for my boys," she had said. I thought it was odd that she called her sons "boys." Lafayette and Gideon were huge! They were old, too, seventeen or eighteen maybe even nineteen or twenty! They weren't married yet, either. I wasn't surprised about that, because they were mean! They laughed at me when I was being serious, and sometimes they flipped my braids. They called me "Cecil" or, even worse,

"Sweetheart!" So I called them "Ratface" and "Ox Ears," but not so Addie could hear me. Maybe she still called them "boys" because those meanies weren't married yet.

"It was a really good bargain," Addie sighed, smoothing the yellow fabric, "But they say they won't wear one stitch of anything I make out of this."

I curled up my lip as I imagined yellow pants. "I don't blame them," I said. "It would be harder to get a girl to marry them if they wear yellow pants. If I saw a man in pants that color, I would look twice. Maybe three times. And not because I would want to marry him, either!"

"Cecilia!" Granny had said, horrified. I scowled. What was wrong with saying what I thought? I didn't want to say "sorry" because I wasn't. I didn't want to hurt Addie's feelings, either, so I went over and felt the yellow cloth between my fingers. It was thick, and had a new fabric stiff feeling. "It feels good and strong," I said in a grown-up voice.

Addie was looking thoughtful. "My husband would have been glad for me to sew him clothes out of this. He was a practical man." I never knew Addie's husband. He'd died before they ever found me in the cabbage patch. I doubted that he would have been glad for yellow pants, either. Unless he was blind.

I glanced at Granny, not saying anything, and put a sad look on my face to show sympathy. I looked at Addie to see if she was crying about her dead husband. She had a faraway, thinking look and a smile on her face! If I'd smiled about a dead person, Granny would have lectured me all day and half the night!

Addie sat up straight. "Well, I'm not going to waste this fabric. If my boys don't want new trousers, I'm going to make me an apron." Addie was a woman of action, like me. A couple of days later, she wore her new apron over to our house. It was big, and had lots of pockets. She kept turning from side to side, making sure we could see all the pockets. She showed us how it tied behind her neck and back with thin strips of yellow fabric folded over several times and sewn into strings. It was a very fine apron. I admired it greatly. It would hold lots of rocks and sticks and bugs.

Addie used her apron pockets all summer to carry picked vegetables from her garden, eggs from the henhouse and tools to work around her place. Addie did a lot of work. Her sons sometimes helped her, but not enough. Grandma said they were "soft." I said they were lazy bums.

Then, at the end of the summer, something got into Addie's henhouse and killed a chicken. I could hear her yelling, "Lafayette! Gideon!" I ran over to her place. She was pretty upset, and I didn't blame her. Chickens were useful. If you got a broody hen that hatched out some chicks, they could get eaten by hawks or dogs or snakes. Then the ones that did live were maybe roosters instead of hens. Hens were better. They laid eggs for a couple of years before they went into the stewpot. You only need one or two roosters in a regular-sized henhouse, so extra roosters were only useful for eating.

"You boys get that rifle fixed!" Addie said, "Some dog or skunk is making a meal of our chickens and I need that rifle to put a stop to it!"

A skunk! Now that was something I'd like to see! Addie kept after her boys, "I asked you before, but you never had time, or you forgot! Today you won't forget! We can't afford to lose any more hens! Now get to town as soon as your chores are done and get Brother Olsen to fix it!"

Fay and Gid looked at each other and raised their eyebrows.

They were up to something. Fay saw me standing there watching. "How's my Cecil today?" he asked with a fake nice voice. I knew it was fake because he knew I hated to be called that name.

I didn't call him Ratface in front of Addie. I stuck my tongue out at him so she couldn't see. I marched home very stiff and proper so they'd know that I knew they were up to something. I heard Gid say, "'Bye, Sweetheart!" and they both started laughing. My face got hot and my teeth got tight together.

A couple of hours later, I saw Ratface and Ox Ears walking past our house toward the center of town. They had the rifle, all right, but they weren't dressed in their working clothes. They looked kind of slick. They were talking and laughing and punching each other on the shoulder. I thought they should punch each other harder. They didn't look very serious to me. They looked like they should both be wearing yellow pants.

They still weren't back when it got dark. I knew Addie had lost her chicken at night. I was wanting to see a real live skunk, so I stepped outside and looked around. A lantern moved from Addie's front door toward the henhouse. In the lantern light, it was easy to see the yellow apron. I didn't tell Granny I was going out because she would say "no." I just started walking toward the lantern. Before I could reach it, it disappeared into the henhouse. I stopped to let my eyes adjust to the dark.

There was a sliver of moon that shone weakly over the yard. I moved slowly closer to the henhouse, feeling my way with my feet. I could hear scrabbling and squawking. "Addie?" I called, but there was no reply.

I was curious as could be, but I figured I'd get in trouble if I opened the door and let any chickens out. I found a small crack in the henhouse door and put my eye to it. I could make out Addie's outline in the lantern light. She was blocking most of my view, holding still, facing the far corner of the henhouse. She stood there for a long time. I couldn't see anything happening, nor could I smell a skunk. I moved my eyes around, trying to see something besides Addie's back.

I was beginning to feel bored until Addie shifted her weight to one side. What I saw then took all my tiredness away and made my breath freeze in my chest. My wide-awake eyes stared at two shiny spots against the far wall. The spots were eyes. Those eyes were stuck in the head of a bobcat!

I wanted to scream, but I couldn't make my mouth do it. Screaming wouldn't have helped Addie, anyway. As I stared at those slitted, cruel eyes, desperately thinking of how I could help, the eyes suddenly sprang straight at Addie! Then I did scream, but so did Addie. The bobcat crashed into the lantern Addie held in her hand, then fell and went out.

I couldn't see anything! Now what should I do? Addie was alone in the dark with a wild bobcat! I strained my eye at the crack. Was she still alive? I was so scared, it felt like the mill wheel was rolling over my chest.

Then I heard Addie muttering, and I started breathing again. She wasn't dead!

She didn't sound scared, she sounded angry! I heard the snarl of an enraged bobcat, and shivered. I heard a chilling yowl, and a scrabbling sound. The yowl turned into a gurgle, and Addie grunted and gasped. Did it have her by the throat? Did I dare open the door? What if it jumped out and got me? What if Addie was dying in there? I had to do something!

My heart thumping like Indian drums, I pulled on the henhouse door and peeked in. I still couldn't see anything.

"Addie?" I called fearfully. I heard heavy breathing. Was it Addie or the bobcat? "ADDIE," I called desperately.

"Open the door," Addie answered shakily. I pulled the door open all the way, dreading what I would see. The thin moonlight leaked into the henhouse, faintly illuminating Addie, sitting on the henhouse floor in the straw with a yellow bundle on her lap. "Oh, Addie, I thought you were dead!"

"Not yet," she said, "*It's* dead." As she stood up on trembling legs, the bundle slid off her lap. I stared in horrible fascination at the head of a bobcat sticking out of Addie's yellow apron, with the strings pulled tightly around his neck. This was way better than a skunk!

"Help me, please," Addie said, and I took her hand and led her out of the coop. After I shut the door I noticed that she was holding her arms out away from her body. "Are you all right?" I asked.

"Got scratched up a bit," she said. I took her into her house and fetched the salve and salt she told me to get. The gashes that crisscrossed her arms and chest were leaking blood.

She told me to sprinkle salt on the wounds, but when I did, she gasped and writhed in so much pain that I stopped. Addie grabbed a handful of salt out of the bag and finished the job, making the most horrible faces, with her teeth showing and her lips pulled back tight, like a skeleton head. Her eyes were so squinted up with pain, they looked closed. I thought she might scream, but she only made pained noises, then said, "liniment" through her closed teeth. I quickly smoothed some liniment over the wounds, and Addie relaxed her face. Then I found three bleeding gashes on her jaw and cheek. She was so brave. I wanted to grow up to be like Addie.

Her two "boys" burst in the door, laughing, no rifle in their hands. When they saw Addie, their laughter turned into a look of horror. "Mother!" Gid cried, "What happened?" He looked at me as though I were to blame. I squinted my eyes at that old Ox Ears so he would know I didn't like his looks.

"You two boys go take a look at the baby doll in the henhouse," Addie replied.

"Is it yours?" Fay said really rudely to me as he and Gid headed for the door. Later Granny said he was rude because he was scared for his mother, which doesn't make any sense.

When they came back in, they looked very white and shocked. "How did you do that?" they asked their mother.

"I had to," she said. "I had no rifle, no knife, no weapon but my hands and my apron. After the bobcat broke the lantern, I figured he'd go for me again. I untied my apron in the dark. The next time he sprang at me, I caught him in the cloth and wound the strings around his neck, then pulled with all my might."

"I'm so sorry about the rifle," said Gid, who looked like he might start to cry. This was interesting.

"We got it there too late to get fixed today," Fay confessed.

"You didn't go straight to the gunsmith, did you, boys?" Addie asked.

"Fay wanted to stop by Larsen's first," Gid blurted out. I knew Larsen's, and they weren't on the way to town. Lucy Larsen was pretty, even though she was old like Addie's boys.

Addie must have noticed the interested look on my face. She said to me, "Does your Granny know you're here?"

I looked at her sideways out of my eyes. "She might."

"I thought so. Now you go on home."

I pulled my bottom lip down with my fingers. Addie said,

"Cissy, I'm tired and need to go to bed. You've been the best help. What would I have done without you?"

"Maybe you would have died," I answered solemnly as I walked over to kiss her good bye. I gave Fay and Gid a haughty look, and said, "I can kill a chicken, but I think it's much better to kill a bobcat with your bare apron strings."

I wanted to stick my tongue out at Ox Ears and Ratface, but I was being mature, so I walked out the door and shut it firmly behind me.

As I began making my way home, I heard Fay and Gid still apologizing to their mother, my friend, the Bobcat Killer.

Adelia Sidwell found a bobcat in her henhouse and strangled it with her apron strings because her two sons had put off getting the broken rifle fixed. She doctored her wounds with salt and homemade liniment. Her sons came home and found their mother scratched and bleeding and the bobcat dead in the henhouse.

Don't Judge A Horse By Its Hide

Ma stacked the dirty breakfast dishes and carried them to the dishpan as Pa scooted his chair back from the table and stood up. With Ma's back turned, I crammed another biscuit into my mouth. The whole thing.

Pa lifted up one corner of his mouth in a small half-smile and shook his head. The half-smile meant that he thought it was kind of funny. The shaking head was for his obligation as a parent to try to teach me some manners. That was Ma's influence.

Pa had not always been the kind of man who needed plates and silverware to eat with. Many times his cup had been the palm of his hand, his eating utensils his own fingers as he filled his calling to help pioneer travelers on their difficult and dangerous journey across the plains and mountains to find a new home in Utah.

I swallowed my biscuit and followed Pa out to the corrals. The sun was brightening the eastern mountain range. Pa leaned against the corral poles and whistled. A plain brown horse, rather on the small side, pricked up her ears and trotted over to him.

"Hello, Flapjack, old girl," Pa said.

My friend Oscar Hakanson had told me he thought Flapjack was a stupid name for a horse. "Don't blame me," I said, "I didn't name her."

It was Ma's idea. She had taken one look at the newborn

colt and said how it was just the color of a golden brown flap-jack. Pa was so smitten with Ma, he'd adopted the name for the little horse. Now he seemed to be nearly as smitten with the homely little horse. He said you can't judge a book by its cover. He claimed she was the smartest horse in Utah Territory.

I thought she was the most unremarkable horse in the Territory, one that I easily overlooked every time. I much preferred to ride Captain, a big bay with a handsome blaze of white streaking down his face and four white socks that lent a flash of distinction to his proud gait.

Pa walked over to the corral gate, Flapjack shadowing him along the fence. She knew what day this was. You could see it in her eager step. Pa saddled and bridled Flapjack while I fed the livestock. Ma came out of the house just then. She carried my 6-year-old brother, his head resting on her shoulder.

"How are you doing, Albert?" Pa asked the little boy. Albert coughed, then held his arms out to Pa who took him and cradled him for a few minutes. At least Albert's fever was down. He still felt weak, which meant I still had to do his chores. Ma had been busy making hot, smelly mustard plasters to stick on Albert's skinny little chest as it heaved with the effort to breathe. I was glad that Albert was breathing easier now, but his cough was still hanging on. I hoped we were all done with the stinking mustard plasters.

Now I would be in charge of Pa's chores, too, while he made his scheduled mail run. Pa handed Albert back to Ma. "Be careful," Ma said as she brushed a kiss across Pa's cheek. "Watch out for Indians."

"We always do," Pa said cheerfully. Pa clapped me on the back before he stepped up into the stirrup and threw his leg over the saddle. Then he was off down the road, trotting at a steady pace. With the mail stops along the way and the distance to Fort Provo, we wouldn't see Pa again until tomorrow evening.

The next night we were eating dinner when we heard Flapjack's hooves drum into the yard. Ma began to set a place for Pa. I went out to help him take care of the horse. When Pa came in, he smiled at the sight of Albert sitting at the table

. The next week, Pa began to cough. It started out mild, but quickly progressed to the deep, rasping cough that had afflicted my brother. The morning of the mail run, Pa was lying in bed, sweat shining on his forehead.

"No!" Ma said, "You can't go!"

"But they're depending on me," Pa said just before he broke into a fit of coughing.

"They'll just have to understand. Some things are more important than the mail," Ma said sternly.

"I've never missed a run yet," Pa said in a raspy voice.

"I know. You are a good man, a man of integrity, but no one expects you to make a mail run in the condition you're in." Ma patted Pa's shoulder. "I'll make you a mustard plaster." Pa groaned.

"I'll go, Pa," I said.

Pa coughed harshly. When he could finally speak, he said, "It's dangerous."

"I can do it." I wanted my Pa to see me as a young man, not a boy. I wanted adventure, a challenge, and I wanted to get away from those smelly mustard plasters.

"If someone has to go, you might as well send Oliver. He's a good hand with horses. You tell him all the stops, give him a blessing, and we'll say a family prayer before he leaves."

That was more than I wanted to take the time to do, especially since Ma had the plaster heating on the stove, and the smell was beginning to turn my stomach. But if that was what it took, I would do it.

I sat on the edge of the bed so my father could place his hands on my head. As he gave me a father's blessing, invoking the powers of heaven for safety on my journey, I felt a warmth on my shoulders as though someone else had placed their hands there. And Pa didn't cough once as he spoke the words of protection and guidance.

Pa laid out the route for me, the places I should stop and the stretches where I should keep out a sharp watch. "Give Flapjack her head," he said.

"But she's so small," I protested, "I thought I would take Captain instead."

Pa shook his head, but couldn't speak because he had a violent fit of coughing. When he finally stopped, he said, "You take Flapjack on the mail run. And remember to give her her head."

I agreed, as it seemed the only way to get Pa's permission to go on this adventure. Did Pa think I was a baby? I knew how to handle horses.

Right after family prayer and before Pa could think of anything else, I went out the door and shut Pa's hoarse coughing and those smelly fumes behind me. Reluctantly, I saddled Flapjack. Just as I threw my leg over the saddle, Ma came out the door. I figured she was going to tell me not to go after all, but instead she handed me a small cloth bundle. The smell of bread and cheese and an apple fritter that she had wrapped up for me to eat on my journey filled my nostrils.

"Thanks, Ma," I said, and turned the horse toward the road.

Ma said, "On your way out, check with the Hakansons and see if one of their boys will look in on us tonight in case Albert and I need help with the chores."

A twinge of guilt tweaked at my heart. I was so anxious to leave, I hadn't even thought what this would do for Ma, having to doctor Pa and do the chores, too. "Yes, Ma," I said meekly.

The Hakanson's assured me that someone would check on my mother. They had a large family, enough to spare. I'd never stopped to count, but it seemed as though they had about a dozen children of all sizes running around. I read what looked like envy in Oscar's face when he found out I was making the mail run. Sitting tall in the saddle, I turned and rode away. I was a free man with an important job to do.

The stops were not hard to find, and there weren't many. Between us and Fort Provo was mostly space. The horse and I soon finished our mail collection and headed across the Sanpete valley toward the mouth of Salt Canyon.

The day had grown hot, and I noticed a pretty little stand of cottonwoods down by the Sanpitch River. The silvery green leaves stirred slightly, beckoning me into their shade. Young green willows filled the gaps between the white trunks with lush, cool leaves. I angled Flapjack toward them welcoming the thought of a respite from the sun by riding through those cool, whispering trees. I was on my own, and was master of my time. I could go where I wanted and not have to get anyone's permission or explain myself. All was right with the world.

Suddenly, Flapjack veered away from the cottonwoods, trotting more briskly than I was asking her to. Stupid horse. She was going to miss those trees by a mile.

She balked as I pulled her head around to face the trees

again, but I was firm. She needed to learn who was the boss. I urged her into a walk and eased up the pressure on the reins, but she veered off track again, and headed for the hot, treeless part of the valley floor.

I gritted my teeth. Captain would have obeyed my commands. He would have gone where I told him to go. Flapjack was just spoiled. Pa probably let her do whatever she wanted to. Well, it wouldn't work that way with me.

I again forced Flapjack's head to turn toward the trees. If she didn't cooperate soon, we would miss the stand and its soothing shade altogether. A hot breeze blew past me and into the arms of the cottonwoods. The silvery green leaves whispered an invitation to me.

Even though her head was pointed toward the trees, Flapjack was sidestepping away from the cooling shade, slowly but surely headed for the open part of the valley floor where the only cover was sagebrush.

"Give her her head."

I whipped around in my saddle to see who had ridden up behind me but I couldn't see anybody. The valley was seemingly empty of people. I wondered at the voice, but didn't feel scared. Maybe it was just a memory of what Pa had told me. Well, who was I to argue with that advice? Flapjack was going to go where she wanted to anyway.

Disgusted, I quit trying to point the little brown horse the way I wanted to go. Shaking my head, I couldn't figure out why Flapjack was Pa's favorite. She wasn't anything to look at, and what good was a horse that didn't do what you wanted it to?

Flapjack was trotting briskly, moving faster than I thought she should go. Distance riding was a matter of pacing. She'd wear herself out.

94

I gathered the reins up, ready to pull her back to a slower pace.

"Give her her head."

I couldn't stop myself from looking behind me again, even though I knew no one was there.

As I turned back to face forward, I noticed the willows between the silvery cottonwood trunks shaking violently. There was hardly any wind. Certainly not enough to account for that much motion. What was going on?

Before my horrified eyes, five Indians riders burst from the innocent looking cover of the willows and galloped toward us, whooping and hollering.

Without any urging from me, Flapjack broke into a gallop. I hung on, my heart racing faster than the little brown horse's hoofbeats.

It wasn't long before Flapjack put a substantial distance between us and the Indians. I was amazed at her speed and endurance. The Indians soon gave up their ambush. Thanks to the plain brown horse, we had been too far away from their hiding place to be taken by surprise.

The next day, after I had recounted my adventures to my worried mother and admiring brother, my Pa said, "I've always thought that little horse can smell Indians. She's gotten me out of more than one scrape with them."

Now Pa and I were in complete agreement. Flapjack was the best horse in Utah Territory.

A father and son team in Spring City used a Morgan cross horse for their leg of the Pony Express route. They claimed the

95

horse could smell Indians, as she always avoided them wherever they lay in wait for the mail riders. The local Indians admired the wily horse so much that it became a game for them to try to ambush the horse and rider. They would rush out from their hiding place, laughing and yelling as they waved at the speedy horse. The Pony Express rider would give a friendly wave in return as the horse galloped away.

She Loves Me, She Loves Me Not

I walked a carefully-measured half-block behind the slender figure limping along the street, thinking of ways I could offer to help her with the heavy burlap sack she carried without sounding too eager. I imagined striding up and saying gallantly, "Allow me," and taking the sack from her hand. Or I could be more direct, "I'll take that now." Or I could try the flattering approach, "That's too heavy for you, let me carry it."

As I played different possibilities over in my head, my mind wandered forward to the day when lovely Mary Artemesia Lowry and I would be married. I could see us riding down the wide main street of Manti in a shiny black carriage—Mr. and Mrs. Piers Madsen. Everyone who saw us would stop and stare in admiration. Most would wave, since we were such a popular and attractive couple. It would be spring, and my lovely bride would slap my face to get the flies off it.

I jumped back as Mary pulled her hand away from my cheek. Her large blue eyes, set in a perfect oval face and framed by glossy black hair, were wide with surprise. "Oh, Piers, I'm sorry!" she laughed, "I was trying to work the kinks out of my back. This potato sack is heavy."

While daydreaming, I hadn't noticed Mary drop her sack, raise her arms above her head, and slowly twist from side to side. I had walked right into her perfect white hand as she was twisting toward me.

I stood staring down at her lovely flushed face. Although I

was fourteen and she was seventeen, I was tall for my age. And she was perfect for hers. Three years was nothing. Once she knew the deep feelings of my heart, she would know that no one could love her like I did, and she would wait for me. She wouldn't be able to help herself.

I had us back in the buggy, heading for the sunset, when she said, "Piers, I know I'm almost home, but would you mind carrying this sack the rest of the way for me?"

I could have stomped on my own toe! Kicked myself! Put my head in a well! What a dunce! I missed a perfect opportunity to offer to carry it for her! "Of course, yes, I'll be most honored to carry it for you, from here to Ephraim if you like, that would be no problem at all!" I babbled. I grasped the sack with both hands and swung it over my shoulder, intending to stand straight and strong as a hardwood tree, but instead, needing to take two steps to catch my balance when that heavy sack thwacked me in the back!

Mary pretended not to notice. "Thank you, Piers," she said sweetly. When we got to her house, she opened the door. I staggered in and she showed me where the kitchen was.

Beside the kitchen doorway sat her old Granny in a rocking chair, a crocheted afghan over her knees. "Hello, Granny," Mary said cheerily and kissed her on the cheek. Her Granny didn't speak or look at Mary. She just stared straight ahead.

"Is she alright?" I asked as I lowered the sack.

"Granny? Oh, yes, of course," Mary said, pulling an apron from a peg and tying it around her small waist. "She just doesn't speak anymore. Pa says she did all her allotted talking in life, and when she'd said it all, she just stopped!" Mary smiled a darling smile at the family joke, but after a moment of silence, she continued more soberly, "Granny doesn't speak or even seem to know we're here. Still, I can't stop myself from speaking to her and giving her a kiss. Maybe she can still feel things." Mary put her small, soft hand on Granny's shoulder. "She doesn't seem to be in pain, and she's such a dear, I'll help take care of her as long as she lives." Mary looked up at me with wet eyes that melted my insides. Confiding her innermost feelings to me swelled my heart with resolve to always protect her from any harm. She smiled and brushed at her eyes with her hand. Then her eyes focused on her sleeve and she said, "Oh, no!"

"What's wrong?" I asked.

"My button is gone!" she said with a note of despair. The end of her sleeve was loose. I could see the smooth, pink, inner part of her wrist as the fabric flopped over with an empty buttonhole dangling about an inch below her arm. The sight of her soft, rosy skin made me breathe faster.

"I'll find it!" I declared, as I strode for the door. I meant to re-trace every step of the way until I found that button. I charged out the door and bumped into Sarah Peacock, Mary's older sister. Her gray eyes and her mouth opened wide in surprise. Her husband, Judge George Peacock, was standing behind her and grabbed her shoulders to steady her. He was a young man for a judge and had a square face and a well-groomed moustache. He said, "Hold on there, now, Son!"

I felt my face grow hot. I wished I were anywhere but here, like Salt Lake City, or Illinois, or maybe even Africa. "I'm so sorry," I said, ducking my head, then trying to turn it into a bow, which didn't work very well. "So very sorry," I mumbled as I looked up and saw Sarah's amused expression. "Excuse me, please," I said as politely as I could through clenched teeth, and I ran down the walkway.

I felt better when I started looking for that button. I was a man on a mission. I spent a lot of time looking. Buttons were scarce in the settlements, and hard to come by.

After what felt like hours of searching, I finally noticed the gray button in the dirt by the spot where Mary had stopped and stretched her arms over her head. I scooped it up like it was a precious diamond, and headed home with it. I decided I would take it to her tomorrow, when I was sure Judge Peacock and Sarah would be gone.

When I woke up the next morning, Mary's button was the first thing I thought of. I felt warm and light headed. When I walked out to the outhouse, I got dizzy. "Ah, true love," I thought to myself.

As I made my way to Mary's house, I wondered if I should put the button in a bunch of flowers, and let Mary find it in there. Would she think that was odd? Would it make her like me better? I could hide it in a piece of my mother's cake. The thought of cake made me gag, and I stopped walking. But what if Mary swallowed the button before she found it? Bad idea. I could tell by the queasiness in my stomach. I began walking again. Maybe I would pretend I hadn't been able to find it, and then pull it out of my pocket at the last minute, just to see her face light up. Maybe she would be so happy and grateful, she would throw her arms around me. Maybe she would kiss me!

Lost in enraptured thoughts, it was only when I was across the street from Mary's that I noticed a tall, old Indian cut across the grass to the Lowry's front door. I knew who he was. He was Chief Walker, the Ute Indian who had invited the settlers to come to Sanpete County many years earlier. Exceptionally tall, he walked with a long stride. I supposed he had dealings of some sort or another with Brother Lowry. But surely he would not be home at this hour. Chief Walker did not hesitate at the door of the Lowry's house. He walked right in.

I kept going, too, but instead of heading for the door, I veered around to a side window and looked in. Things around me looked sort of foggy. I felt like I was in a dream. I wiped my sweating forehead and focused on Mary standing on a chair. It looked like she had been surprised in the act of putting something away up on a high shelf. She was shaking her head and pointing toward the door. I heard Chief Walker say, "No. I come see you."

Mary stepped down from the chair and walked quickly toward the kitchen. Chief Walker followed her. I couldn't see them anymore, so I sneaked toward the back of the house.

I wasn't sure what to do. I didn't know what Chief Walker wanted. He could be nice to the settlers, or he could be nasty. It all depended on his mood. He had been baptized a member of the Church of Jesus Christ of Latter-day Saints, but he was also still taking slaves and occasionally killing rival tribal members, as well as stealing cattle and horses. He was just plain unpredictable. I had to protect Mary. I knew I was no match for a full-grown Indian who had lived a warrior life, but I had to watch over Mary. If necessary, I would die for her.

I could imagine my funeral. All the girls in the settlement would be there, crying over my coffin, and the Bishop would say, "This boy is bound for the Celestial Kingdom. Greater love hath no man than that he lay down his life for his brother..."

I felt a sudden jolt as my leg sank into the ground. I fleetingly wondered if I had stepped into my grave, but a painful wrench in my knee let me know I was still very much alive. The jolt left me feeling woozy. I looked around the yard through watering eyes. It looked as though I had stepped into a hole that had been dug to set a clothesline pole. I could also see that I was very near an open kitchen window. As I dragged my leg out of it's little would-be grave, I heard Chief Walker say,

"...and you have teepee here, in town. No go in mountains with other squaws. Give you many best furs, ermine, beads, a fine horse. You have all you want."

I pulled myself up by the window ledge and looked in just as Mary answered, "I can't marry you."

I almost lost my hold on the ledge! Chief Walker was asking her to MARRY him? This was like a very bad dream. I could see Mary standing behind her grandmother's rocking chair, alternately placing her hands on the old woman's shoulders and on the back of the chair as though she couldn't find a comfortable place to rest them.

"Why?" Chief Walker boomed in a challenging voice. It sounded like he was far away.

Mary jumped, then straightened her spine into a stiff line. "Because I'm already married," she declared.

Now I knew this was a really bad dream! Chief Walker and I must have had similar looks of disbelief and dismay on our faces as we stared at her. Chief Walker broke the silence first. "WHO?" he bellowed. He stabbed a large hunting knife into the wooden kitchen table. It stood upright, quivering, as he challenged Mary with a steely stare.

She hesitated. I held my breath. My head was pounding, and it felt like fog was moving in over my eyes. I squinted to see better. "Judge George Peacock is my husband," she said.

Walker grabbed his knife, wrenched it from the table, and stalked out of the house. I moaned in pain, pain of the body and pain of the heart. In her hour of need, she had not thought of me, she had thought of her brother in law! It was more than my love-burst heart could take. Everything faded into black.

When I woke up, I was at home, in my bed. At first I was relieved. It had only been a dream. A bad dream. A very bad dream. "So they've gone off to Salt Lake," I heard my Aunt Martha say. I vaguely wondered who had gone to Salt Lake.

"Well, but it was the only thing for it," my mother replied. "Brother Lowry was right"

Lowry? Mary? My heart skipped a beat. "Mother?" I called.

"Piers!" she exclaimed, and bustled over to my side. "You had me so worried! Why didn't you tell me you had a fever? You shouldn't have gone out! Didn't you feel dizzy and weak? What were you thinking about? Brother Lowry found you lying by his house and thought you were dead!"

"Lowry," I said.

"Yes," interrupted Aunt Martha, coming up beside Mother, "You were at the Lowry's." She spoke slowly, as though I were a small child.

"I know," I said impatiently, "Where's Mary?"

"Gone to Salt Lake," said Aunt Martha slowly and distinctly.

"Why?" I asked.

"Well, that's the exciting part of the story," Aunt Martha spoke faster as she warmed up to her gossip, "See, Chief Walker asked Brigham Young if he could marry a white woman. President Young said if the woman agreed, it would be all right. So the Chief had the gall to ask Mary Lowry to marry him! Imagine! I shudder at the thought. She, of course, would have nothing to do with that. Yet that clever girl knew if she turned him down, he might take offense and retaliate on the town. Who knows what atrocities would have been rained down on our heads! That brave girl thought to tell that savage that she was already married, and to Judge George Peacock, too! That sent Chief Walker back into the mountains. When Mary's father came home and she told him what happened, he said she had to marry the judge to make good on her word to Chief Walker, so they hitched up their buggy and went to Salt Lake City to get married. Isn't it romantic?"

"Oh!" I moaned. I had never minded the thought of plural marriage until this moment. It was perfectly legal for Judge Peacock to be married to Sarah and then marry Mary, too, as long as both women agreed.

I couldn't understand how Mary could be content to live without me. I carried her potato sack for her, and even found her button! But I'd never given it to her. If I had, she would have known how much I was willing to sacrifice for her happiness. Now it was too late. She was gone from me forever. All I had left was her button, which I decided I would always keep close to me. She could get a new one while she was in Salt Lake City.

I recovered slowly from my fever. In January, Chief Walker died. Some people said it was from a broken heart. I believed it.

Chief Walkara got permission from Mormon Church president Brigham Young to marry a white woman provided he found one who would agree to marry him.. He proposed to young Mary Artemesia Lowry. Fearing for the safety of the town if she refused, she told him she was already married. When he stabbed his knife in the table and asked "Who?" all she could think of was her brother-in-law Judge George Peacock. Walkara left in a temper. When Mary told her father the story, he sent Mary and George to Salt Lake as quickly as possible to be married. Chief Walkara died the following January.

About the Author

Shirley Anderson Bahlmann was born in Logan, Utah, and spent her childhood in Haddon Heights, New Jersey. She is fourth in a family of six girls and two boys, a red-haired mother and a harmonica-playing father.

When she was twelve, her family moved to Manti, Utah. Music, writing, English, and drama were her favorite school subjects. She wrote her first novel when she was ten years old. She enjoyed French class in junior high, journalism in high school, and editing the Snow College newspaper during her sophomore year there.

She also kept busy playing saxophone in the jazz band, winning the Miss Snow College crown, and meeting her tall, dark, and handsome husband, Robert.

Over the years she has written road shows, skits, family plays, and freelance material for friends and local newspapers.

Shirley has always had a fascination for old houses, buildings, and ghost towns. Being of old pioneer stock, she has a natural curiosity about the people who actually settled in western United States. She also feels fortunate to have perspective from new pioneers, since her husband is the son of Dutch immigrants.

Shirley and Robert are the proud parents of six sons—Andy, Jeff, Scott, Zackary, Brian, and Michael—whose ages span twenty years. The three youngest still live at home.

If you have an inspiring, unusual, humorous, or just plain interesting true story, please send it to me at:

Shirley Bahlmann
PO Box 33
Manti, Utah 84642

Or e-mail me: **yoshirley@yahoo.com**

CEDAR FORT, INCORPORATED
Order Form

Name:_____

Address: _____

City: _____ State: _____ Zip: _____

Phone: ( ) _____ Daytime phone: ( ) _____

Against All Odds

Quantity: _____ @ $10.95 each: _____

plus $3.49 shipping & handling for the first book: _____

(add 99¢ shipping for each additional book)

Utah residents add 6.25% for state sales tax: _____

TOTAL: _____

Mail this form and payment to:

Cedar Fort, Inc.

925 North Main St.

Springville, UT 84663

You can also order on our website **www.cedarfort.com**

or e-mail us at sales@cedarfort.com or call 1-800-SKYBOOK

9 26575 75902 3